i'm just getting to the disturbing part

on work, fear and fatherhood

steven church

Outpost19 | San Francisco
outpost19.com

Church, Steven
        I'm Just Getting to The Disturbing Part/ Steven
Church
        ISBN: 9781944853457 (pbk)

Library of Congress Control Number: 2018935364

OUTPOST19

ORIGINAL
PROVOCATIVE
READING

i'm just
getting
to the
disturbing
part

To my parents, all of them teachers.

2017 | FRESNO ——————

1995 | BRECKENRIDGE ——————

1996 | FLAGSTAFF ——————
1996 | BRECKENRIDGE ——————

1998 | FORT COLLINS ——————

2000-2002 | FORT COLLINS ——————

2002 | POUDRE CANYON ——————

2004 | FORT COLLINS ——————

2005 | PAWTUCKET ——————

2006 | FRESNO ——————

2005-2007
PAWTUCKET | FRESNO ——————

2011 | FRESNO ——————

Preface:
Against Clarity

I've attended a lot of public readings given by writers of poetry, fiction, and nonfiction. I've seen a lot of wonderful, inspiring, thought-provoking, and emotionally powerful readings; and I've also seen a lot of very very bad readings. But I've only booed one writer in my life.

I was a thirty-year-old graduate student, taking my first tentative steps into being a writer of literary nonfiction, memoir, and personal essay. I'd recently given up fiction writing and was working on a memoir, a manuscript that would end up being my first book. The visiting writer was a fairly well-known author who toured widely, and he was in town supporting his recently published book. I hesitate to say more than this about his work, if only because then it would be easier to identify this individual, and this isn't really about him, but instead about what he represents.

This writer was paid, probably not a lot of money, but more certainly than I was making in a month as a graduate student TA; and he was paid to come and talk with students about writing. He was paid to inspire and encourage them.

So this writer read his work. I didn't care much for it, but I kept quiet. Then he asked the audience for questions; and in response to one I can't recall, he stood there at the podium, all puffed up and pompous, and told us all that, "nobody should be allowed to write personal essays or memoir until they've reached the age of 45 and achieved clarity."

This is when I did it.

I cupped my hands to my mouth and yelled, "Boooooooo!" as other people applauded.

Audience members turned and stared.

"Bullshit," I muttered.

It also helped, according to him, if you'd done something really exciting and story-worthy like he'd done when he drove a motorcycle across the country. The message was loud and clear. I didn't know shit. I had no "right" to write about anything because, apparently, I hadn't earned my license. Hell, I'd have to wait another 15 years before I could even start writing.

I wondered if my "clarity" would come on suddenly, like a hot flash or a sneeze, maybe like a really long orgasm. And when would he mail me my laminated "writing license"? Wouldn't they need a picture and my height and weight? Is there some kind of multiple choice test? I had so many questions.

So after the reading, I approached the writer and introduced myself, "Hi, I'm Steven. I'm a 30-year-old memoirist."

Fortunately, I'm distrustful of fundamentalism in all forms and I immediately knew that I wasn't going to listen to this writer, and further that my frustration and distrust wasn't even so much with him personally but with the ideas about writing nonfiction that he represented. To me, he got it all wrong. There was no private club, no privileged position you had to earn before you could write. Or if there was, I wanted to kick the door in and take over the joint.

I'm now 46 years old, still kicking at doors, and wondering when the promised clarity might show. I'm anxiously awaiting some kind of "writing license," hoping they can use my latest author photo where the black-and-white exposure makes me look older and wizened and full of clarity, the kind of guy who is worthy of writing memoirs and personal essays. In the meantime, I've published two memoirs and four collections of essays and now I'm editing a whole anthology of essays—which I guess is sort of like driving around without a license and hoping I don't get caught.

I guess I'm still waiting for clarity to arrive, like a gift I wake up to on Christmas morning, and suddenly everything will make sense. But most of the time, I hope that it never comes and that life continues to be a crazy chaotic mess of surprises, that it is consistently unpredictable, and I thus have reason to continue writing. For me nonfiction writing—memoir and personal essay—has never been about clarity, which seems not only highly overrated as a state of mind, but also anathema to the origins of the essay, which saw the form as an exercise in self-doubt and noble confusion.

In other words, as I've now entered the vaunted Age of Clarity, I realize that I don't actually want it. Take it. You can have it. And maybe that's the most disturbing part of what that writer said—that false promise of clarity, which to me is just as much a lie as closure or any other posture of reflective control. And if that same writer—now more wizened with age—stood up before an audience of my students and said the same sort of things, I might boo him all over again. I'd tell him that there is a kind of clarity that can exist no matter what your age and experience, that it doesn't matter what you've done, because you don't have to earn your license to write or to think deeply about the world. I'd tell him that my children are smarter than him or me most days; and I'd tell him all that matters is that you're curious about the world, interested in thinking deeply about your experience with it, and capable of sharing that thinking with an audience.

In a May, 2015 piece in the New York Times titled, "Should There Be a Minimum Age to Write Memoir," Leslie Jamison, author of the bestselling and award-winning essay collection, *The Empathy Exams*, says:

> Of course someone will look back at his first broken heart with a different perspective at the age of 40, or 60, or 80. But that doesn't mean that these perspectives are better, or that our self-understanding travels toward some telos of perfect consummation with every passing year. The narratives we tell about our own lives are constantly in flux; our perspectives at each age are differently valuable. What age gains in remove it loses in immediacy: The younger version of a story gets told at closer proximity, with more fine-grain texture and less aerial perspective.

The essays collected here in, "I'm Just Getting to the Disturbing Part" are essays that I mostly wrote long ago, well before I approached the Age of Clarity, and they exhibit, I hope, a kind of clarity of the moment that I could not achieve now, some twelve to fifteen to twenty years later, no matter how hard I tried. They are, I believe, more "textured" and less "aerial" in their perspective; and I hope they also achieve a clarity of purpose and language, even embracing the truth that, "the narratives we tell about our own lives are constantly in flux."

These essays are essays that have, for whatever reason, resisted being incorporated or absorbed into other books, perhaps because there is something uniquely self-contained about each piece, or because they were a kind of outlier to the main threads in a book, sort of like the b-sides to a record album, which we all know were sometimes better than the a-sides, but harder to describe and market. Often times these essays simply resisted being revised and re-envisioned through that more distant, aerial perspective. In some cases, they represent my first sustained and successful efforts to write about material that has since shown up again and again in other work; and as such, they capture a truth of those experiences, one that is more immediate and unmediated, one that would be lost if seen through the lens of clarity, years removed from the events.

The title essay, "I'm Just Getting to the Disturbing Part," has been anthologized and read widely, and I've tried for years to work it into different book manuscripts; but this essay in particular has a kind of stubborn youthful resilience to it that refuses to bend or break or become anything other than what it is. And while I've made minor edits to some of the pieces in here, mostly for the sake of consistency, they are largely in the same form in which they were published originally, in small literary magazines. My hope is that these essays explore and illuminate, if only for a few moments on the page, some truths about my life and the wider world, even if these truths are constantly in flux; because one truth is that I'm always, it seems, just getting to the disturbing part.

Deep Down in the Country Boy Mine

BREATHING BENEATH THE SURFACE

This is what things have come to: I am a tour guide at the Country Boy Gold Mine. I have a lot of responsibility. I help people breathe. And I get paid to tell them stories. First thing in the morning, I crank up the vent fan in the Portal and let it run for a couple of hours. The fan is attached to a large yellow nylon bag that snakes down the length of the tunnel, feeding fresh air to the far reaches of the mine. With the fan going the bag shudders and vibrates with breath. It seems almost alive. But some afternoons, even after we've run the pump all morning, the air at the back starts to get thin and I have to take deep sucking breaths. It's even worse for the guests. Some of them turn green and drop like trapped flies. They just aren't prepared for life underground.

At the end of my tour, I line everyone up, switch off the lights, and show them how dark it can get 1000 feet underground, how dark it must have been for the old miners. I keep a prop-candle in the front pocket of my coveralls; but sometimes when I try to light it, there's not enough oxygen to keep a flame. Even fire can't breathe; and in those brief moments of distraction or reflection, the candle flickering faintly blue, sputtering to survive underground, I might think about the girl I left 600 miles away and how terrified I am of losing her.

1

SHOW AND TELL

This is 1995 and I want to be a mountain man, a pioneer of sorts. I have a BA in philosophy. I am a member of the esteemed academic honor society, Phi Beta Kappa; and I have turned down scholarship offers to study ethical theory in PhD programs and abandoned my girlfriend to come and work as a tour guide and general laborer for the Country Boy Mine in Breckenridge, Colorado[1].

I might be making some really bad decisions.

I'm not alone up here in the rarified air near the Continental Divide. I want what a lot of young men

---

[1]   Country Boy Mine Sample Script for Tour Guides
The Surface: Country Boy Portal

My name is (*Your Name Here*) and I'll be your guide today. I'd like to welcome you the Country Boy and mention a couple of things before we enter the Portal (*Talk with loud voice and enunciate clearly. Smile a lot. Act happy. Try not to think about the phone call last night from her.*) We're standing at 10,500 feet above sea level. You may have felt the burn in your lungs when you walked up from the parking lot. First things first. A few terms you might want to know. (*You did not abandon her. This is just something you have to do. It's about you as a person, as an individual. It's about you as a man.*) In the mine you're *underground*. Out here, where you're standing now, we call this the *surface*. That's the *portal* (*Point at gaping tunnel mouth, a hole in the earth.*) You might notice the long yellow air bag extending down the tunnel. (*Point to yellow nylon air-bag. It looks like some kind of bright bulbous intestine.*) Every morning we turn on the fan and blow fresh air into the back of the tunnel—just so we'll all be able to breathe when we get to the end of the tour. The tunnel climbs slightly uphill and, by 4:00, most of the air will leak out to the surface. Sometimes it's hard to catch your breath, but you'll see what I mean. (*At the end of the day sometimes it feels like you're suffocating without her and you just want to sit there in the absolute darkness, wheezing and coughing like a lonely Old Miner. Jesus, you are pathetic.*)

here are socialized to want—freedom, friends, beer, sports, and fun. No marriage. No family. Maybe a wood-heated log cabin, a Husky mutt dog, and a wild and bushy beard.

I can't grow a beard, and our apartment doesn't allow dogs, but I feel lucky to have landed the job at the Country Boy. It seems to fit my search for identity better than slinging t-shirts at "Shirt and Ernie's" where my roommates both work. At least I'll be in the mountains, out of the city, working hard, telling stories. At least I'll be busy and won't have so much time to think about what I'm leaving behind.

It's funny what people expect from me. I'm not a miner with an engineering or geology degree as many visitors assume. I'm a tour guide with a five-year philosophy degree who turned down PhD programs in California and Connecticut to come to the mountains, live in a bunker-like cinder-block apartment with old friends from high school, smoke dope, and snowboard.

I am not an authority. But I must act like one.

I get paid eight bucks an hour to lead groups of tourists 1000 ft. into the side of a mountain[2] and tell

2   Quick and Dirty History

Before we go underground I'll ask you all to take a look around you and imagine this entire valley buzzing with activity. At the turn of the century, French Gulch was the sight of numerous mining operations, which all but destroyed the natural beauty of the area, reducing the stream to a weak-hearted trickle and covering the valley with enormous piles of rock and tailings. Sluice boxes were built in the creek bed and giant hydraulic cannons pummeled the hillsides while miners swarmed about, digging and panning for gold in the rush of rock and dirt. The quaking aspen groves you

see—which turn a bright gold color in the fall—are the result of mining activities. (*You might say* beauty birthed from devastation, *but be careful not to alienate your guests with high-brow language.*) A scrub

3

tales of the Old Miners and Breckenridge's glorious mining past. It's a pretty cool job and nowhere near as dangerous—or as fulfilling I suppose—as actually mining something of value from this hardrock place.

---

tree, the aspen grows in rocky soil where evergreens won't take hold. They grow best on denuded hillsides and that's why you see them blanketing French Gulch. (*You should probably stop short of saying something about how their beauty thrives on destruction. Opportunistic beauty. Parasitic beauty. Something good growing from something bad. That should be a lesson or something. But not the kind of insight you want to share with the tourists.*) In fact many of the gulches around the Blue River Valley have been the sight of heavy mining activity. You can't climb a ridge without finding abandoned mine shafts and core drilling holes. The town of Breckenridge was a booming gold rush town with a very active red light district. (*Wink knowingly at nearest male.*) When the price of gold plummeted, the miners left and so did everyone else. Breckenridge, like many other mining towns, nearly died. Of course Breck is still populated by miners, but now we dig for tourist dollars instead of the gold stuff (*Laugh heartily. This encourages others to do so and makes it seem as if you're having fun leading them around like a pack of sheep.*) If you'll follow me, we'll start the tour.

DOWN TIME AT THE COUNTRY BOY MINE

Outside the tunnel, on the surface, the mountain air is crisp, cold, and laced with the scent of pine[3]. I'm filling gold pans with dirt, waiting for the tourists to arrive, disgorge from their SUV's, and stream up the hill in breathless hordes, wads of money clutched in their fists.

Jumper, the miniature burro is restless and skitters around on the rocks. He follows me around, nipping at my gloves and occasionally turning around and threatening me with a kick. I just smack him on the rump and shove him aside. I like Jumper. He has personality.

Whitey the sheep, on the other hand, is always stinky wet and smells like an old gym sock. His lips are pink and his tongue hangs out, lolling around grotesquely. He's sort of obscene. He's only a sheep, but he has this way about him—as if he wouldn't mind being taken out behind the shed by a couple of lonely drunken hillbillies.

_____

3   Canary in a Hard Rock Mine

(*Point out canary on your way into the Portal. Try to incorporate into introductory remarks in Dry Room.*) You may have noticed our canary as you entered the mine. Canaries were used in coal mines as detectors of lethal gasses. If the canary dropped dead, the miners knew it was time to get out. Now that I mention it, the little guy doesn't look so great. (*Try to act genuinely concerned. Wait for one of the tourists to look concerned too. Hold for dramatic pause.*) Of course hard rock mines like the Country Boy do not produce lethal gasses. Thus, our canary is merely for show (*and because tourists would demand to see a damn canary if we didn't have one*). Don't let its lifelessness bother you. (*Don't let its lifelessness remind you of something. It doesn't matter if you feel like the canary some days—perched up in a cage, pretending to be normal and happy and yellow.*)

5

Nobody really likes Whitey.

Jumper, however, is a rock star. All the tourists want to pet him and feed him and tug on his ears and scratch his nose. He seems so cute and quaint to them. He's small, about the size of a large dog, but he has an ornery streak, a bitchy side too. He'll nip at people sometimes and shove kids with his nose. I worry occasionally that he might brain a toddler with one swift and violent kick to the head; so I watch him vigilantly, warning guests to avoid his backside.

Despite what appears to me to be a huge liability issue, Jumper's popularity gives Doug the idea to start breeding miniature burros and keeping them at the mine. One of my jobs was to build a shed for Jumper out of lodge-pole pine logs. Soon enough they have four or five burros running around at any given time.

The best mornings at the Country Boy leave me with a few spare minutes, some down time to sit on a log bench and watch the sun climb up over the Continental Divide and spread its color and heat down French Gulch. I love to watch the light slide across the landscape, how the aspens and lodge-pole pines, even the rocks, seem to wait, pausing in suspended animation, then suddenly switch-on with color and burst awake.

Doug and Betsy bought the Country Boy about four years before I started working here. He quit a job as an investment banker in New York, gave up a six-figure salary, and dragged Betsy away from teaching to move to Breckenridge and open the Country Boy.

I ask Doug about this one day and he tells me that when he traveled all over the world for his father's Air Force career, he visited a salt mine in Salzburg, Austria, and never forgot it. Doug's voice cracks and breaks with excitement as he recounts the family trip to the Salt Mine—especially the part where he gets to slide down some kind of salt tunnel. He simply wanted to recreate that sort of experience for tourists in Colorado—so much so that he already has grand ideas of building a massive tunnel-slide on the property.

"I'm thinking it's going to have to be on the surface," he says. "I was hoping we could do something like that in the mine; maybe find an upper tunnel or a shaft." Doug's voice sort of trails off wistfully and I can see that he is lost in the dream.

Doug never stops working to make it a reality. Ever. He lives to work. Tall and thin with unruly hair, he's always confident, always upbeat, never openly worried about anything—business, progress, cave-ins, etc. But he also has a way of looking right through me sometimes, as if I'm just a spare part in a machine he's trying to fix. Doug is one of those dreamers and schemers, never satisfied with one thing, one project, one hobby or habit—eternally spiritually restless.

I spend much of my time at the Country Boy with Betsy, perhaps the most optimistic and positive person I've ever met. She'd have to be. She's bouncy and wide-eyed with a Gidget-sort of demeanor and voice. I always enjoy talking with her. She's been living with Doug in one of the old mouse-infested mining cabins (only recently moving into a house), spends most of her waking hours at the mine, handling the finances or guiding tours; and she never complains, never gets angry, at least not to me. But there are days when I see this mountain life wearing on her, beating her down a bit. I see it in her eyes and the droop of her mouth or the sag of her shoulders.

During breaks between tours, Betsy and I will sit and listen to the radio and talk about the larger world and the smaller worries of living in a mountain town. She's also the only person in Colorado who ever asks me about my girlfriend back home. She'll sit there on a wooden stump-stool for a half-hour or more and listen to me tell her about a phone conversation I had the night before.

When Doug and Betsy bought the Country Boy it was literally a caved-in portal and some ramshackle outbuildings. I can't imagine what she must have thought; standing there on a tailings pile four years ago, looking at this crumbling mountainside, trying to see whatever it was that Doug saw, trying to dream what he dreams.

Now they have a 1000 ft. long tunnel[4], the yellow air

---

4   Brass Tags

You may have noticed hanging below the stuffed canary something called the Tag Board. (*Point out Tag Board. Stand near it.*) Every miner had a brass tag with his name or a number imprinted on it. (*Hold* bag, a gold-panning stream, a museum/gift shop, and a teetering blacksmith shop that, while quite sturdy, looks just minutes from collapsing; and they have dreams of more—shared dreams, I suppose—the kind of stuff that bonds two people forever. It's a quite a spread, a true testament to their marriage.

They both work crazy hard—as if possessed or consumed by these dreams. They're in this thing together—sink or swim—and it's good for me to be around them. I'm almost always busy doing something that requires great mental focus and concentration or great physical exertion. Either way it keeps my mind occupied or my body busy with other pursuits. I've learned quickly here that it's one thing to talk about the holes in your life, and something completely different to give guided tours of them for strangers.

---

up a sample tag.) They carried these with them at all times. It was their pass into and out of the mine. At the end of a shift, if a tag was missing, the mine foreman immediately knew who it was and where he had been assigned to work that day. If a tag was out, it usually meant someone was dead. Now, we don't have enough tags for all of our visitors, so we'll have to rely on the Buddy System. (*You might be tempted here to say something about the tag-board in your girlfriend's heart and how your brass tag is missing, gone, dead—but this seems a bit melodramatic and sentimental for a tour guide. You probably want to avoid those sorts of statements. Just keep those things to yourself and count heads. Always take a count. You don't want to leave someone behind.*)

Our neighbor, Buck, lives in one of the old mining cabins that B&B Mining leases out. Even though they're not actively mining in French Gulch, B&B hangs onto the property—just in case the price of gold should skyrocket again. The cabins don't have running water or electricity. Some of them are barely inhabitable. But there's a whole subculture of people who live in the Gulch and work construction jobs, drive a snow-cat, or run a chair-lift at the resort. They live in these old cabins for next-to-nothing in exchange for "keeping an eye on things."

Buck keeps an eye on the property that borders the Country Boy. But he takes his job a little too seriously sometimes. My roommate Rob once ran across him while riding his bike. Buck crept out of the woods carrying a rifle and confronted Rob for trespassing. Fortunately Buck's bark is a lot worse than his bite and he's easily intimidated. Rob confused Buck with a simple question. He asked him why he had covered the end of his gun-barrels with masking tape, and Buck launched into a rambling explanation about how it keeps him from getting dirt in the gun when he's crawling in the woods, sneaking up on trespassers, etc. When he got home from his ride, Rob told us the story and summed it up with, "He's fucking nuts."

It's true. Buck dresses entirely in buckskin and has a shaggy brown beard that hasn't seen a pair of clippers in years. His hide-pants are shiny with grease and overuse. I often see him at the sandwich bar in King Soopers wearing a large bowie knife, a gun, and a cell phone strapped to his belt. He looks a little crazy, completely out of context; and as you might imagine, Buck smells like someone who dresses entirely in buckskin and lives in a cabin with no running water or electricity. "Gamey" or "pungent" would be the nice way to put it.

I'm also pretty sure that Buck isn't his real name—just some kind of mountain man appellation he adopted to fit his finely crafted image. His real name is probably Marlon or Lars and he grew up in the suburbs of Newark. There's part of me that wants to get to know Buck and talk long into the night about the good full life of a solitary mountain man, about the women and family he left behind. I want to listen to his stories about trapping game and stitching his own clothes from an animal he killed with his bare hands. But there's another part of me that's deeply afraid of Buck—not that he'll hurt me—afraid that he'll ruin the dream and tarnish my fantasy even further.

One day I see him coming up the gravel path just as I'm getting a group of tourists settled in around the gold panning stream and showing them how to work the material around with the water to separate out the gold[5].

---

5   Stop One: The Dry Room

We're still not underground yet, folks. You're standing now in the Dry Room. This is where the Old Miners would have dressed for the day of work and undressed when they were done. The Old Miners wore company issued coveralls along with their hardhats to prevent them from hiding gold in their own clothes. I won't make you change into coveralls but you will have to wear a hardhat for safety purposes. (*You should know that this is where some big-haired women may refuse to wear the helmet. This is also where you get to act like a badass and tell her that if she doesn't wear the helmet, then she can hang out on the surface with Whitey the pervert sheep.*) Help yourself to a hardhat. You can adjust with the dial on the back to fit. They're all the same size.

Doug catches up with Buck just as he's approaching the tourists.

"Hey, Buck," Doug says, slapping him on the shoulder. "How's things?" I'm glad Doug is there to intercept him.

"Crazy, man," Buck says, stopping to stroke at his beard. "Someone sabotaged my truck."

"What?"

"Yeah, they loosened my lug nuts, man. I was driving down to work the other morning and my left front wheel just comes off and rolls out ahead of me."

"You're kidding."

"No way, man. I put the truck in a ditch. Smacked my head real good on the windshield." Buck lifts his hat and pulls his hair back to show a red welt on his forehead. "Messed up my leg a little bit too."

"Sabotage, huh?" Doug says,

"I know it was," Buck says. "Goddamn punk kids. Probably the ones I chased off my property last week."

"Didn't I see you working on your truck last week?" Doug asks. "In fact, weren't you changing the tires?"

"I tightened those fucking bolts," Buck barks indignantly.

"Buck!" Doug hisses, gesturing toward the tourists. "Watch your mouth, OK?"

"Yeah sure, whatever," he says and shuffles down to

(*Of course your girlfriend would never balk at wearing a hardhat. She'd wear the boots and the coveralls. You've seen her ripping asphalt shingles from a roof and working a nail gun like a pro. She'd probably muck like a champ. But she isn't a member of this tour group. She is home, taking classes, partying with friends. She is already refusing to visit you here and there's not a goddamn thing you can do about it.*) There's nothing we can do about it. It's a matter of safety and preparedness. Country Boy Mine is always concerned with Safety and Preparedness.

12

the stream. Buck picks up a pan and walks right out into the water. I look up at Doug and he just smiles. Buck crouches down in the stream and begins to instruct the two kids next to him how to properly swirl the water in their pans such that they won't lose any gold. "No, it's like this," he says.

I watch him, worried what the parents might think; but they're gazing at Buck with a bemused look on their faces. Tourists absolutely love Buck—at least from a distance. He seems so mythical to them, straight out of a storybook. He's not bizarre, he's *eccentric*. He's not stinky and dirty, he's *seasoned* and *weathered*. The way they fawn over him, I know they will tell stories of Buck when they leave this place. I know he'll make a bigger impression on them than I ever will. I'd say we should pay him to hang around the Country Boy, but he's a paranoid misogynistic misanthrope who smells like swamp ass; and once the reality of Buck inevitably clashed completely with the storybook picture of Buck, I don't think the tourists would find him so romantic.

SIDETRIP

One of my first weeks on the job, Doug encourages me to explore the right-hand tunnel, the one we've roped off from the tourists.

"Is it safe?" I ask.

"Sure," he says. "I mean we haven't excavated it or put timber-sets up or anything, but the chance of a cave-in is pretty slim."

"Slim, huh?"

He hands me a flashlight. "It's fun," he says, grinning.

I take the flashlight and make my way into the tunnel. It's my time living and working away from home, and here I am crawling into an abandoned mine-tunnel. What the hell am I doing? I guess it just seems like something I *should* do. Why? I can't really say for sure. Perhaps because it feels adventurous, a once-in-a-lifetime experience, the sort of thing I'll tell my grandkids about. Maybe I'm just stupid.

By the time I reach the rope barrier at the end of the main tunnel, I've talked myself in and out of going several times. But I unclip the rope and step past it, crawling over a small pile of rock. I'm up to my ankles in orange sludge when I reach the end of the lights. Because of all the iron in the rock, the mud in the tunnel is a thick butterscotch orange color and seems especially sticky. The water, of course, is the same color and I hate to think how it might taste—certainly nothing like butterscotch, probably more like iodine. I look back briefly and then just keep going. It's amazing how quickly the light dwindles to a faint glow and it's only my flashlight that keeps me going. The water continues to rise and I have to climb over several other piles of rock. The tunnel keeps getting shorter and shorter until I have to crouch down to avoid hitting my head[6].

Standing there in that hole in the mountain, up to my knees in iron-rich water, between a couple of moldy ancient timbers,[7] I imagine what it would be like to be

---

6   Fun with Dioramas

Now that we're all wearing our grey helmets and looking quite spiffy, I'd like to have you take a look at the diorama behind me. This is a model of the Country Boy. The main tunnel at the Country Boy is a crosscut tunnel. See the way it cuts crossways into the side of the mountain. (*See the way it pulls you from her.*) First they drilled from the top of the ridge and took a core sample (Point to the top of the ridge in the model and trace finger down path of vertical shaft). In the gift shop we have long cylinders of stone, old core samples you folks might want to take a look at later. They'd comb over the ridges around here, plumbing down into the rock, looking for the telltale soft spot of a vein. When their core drill hit one, they blasted a crosscut tunnel up to it, working any other veins they found along the way, and dug a vertical shaft through the vein up to the surface. As I've said, the main tunnel runs just slightly uphill, so that the water always runs out of the tunnel, back to the surface. It's strange, I know, for there to be water in the tunnel. It doesn't make sense. Where's it coming from? And it's equally strange to be underground and think of the surface as being downhill. But that's the way it is in the Country Boy. (You want to avoid thinking about too many strange things. You want to reassure them that there's nothing strange about walking uphill into the side of a mountain, nothing abnormal about a man leaving his girlfriend to lead strangers into a giant hole in the earth).

7   Stop Two: Cross-Timbers

We've stopped here to show you an original set of supporting cross-timbers, most likely lodge-pole pine. This set of timbers is probably 75-100 years old and, as you can see, covered with a thick wet-black mold. Today we build them out of 8X8 Douglas fir;

trapped here. My anxiety fires up like a gas furnace. What if there was a cave-in that sealed off my exit? Some of that rock looks pretty fresh. How long would it take Doug to realize I was missing? What if he never did?

I start to panic, sucking in huge wasteful breaths of air, panting like a dog. But then I realize that my air could run out and I immediately try to slow my lungs. I backpedal, stumbling through the water, and scramble over the piles of rock to get out. I slog through the muck, ducking rock and whacking my helmet a few times, but finally make it back to the new timber sets and the electric lights and sweet familiar safety.

I sit down next to the switch, reach up, pop off the glow, and pause there in the absolute darkness, waiting for my heart to calm down. As jacked as I am, there's something soothing about this moment—probably an analgesic rush of adrenaline, the kind of sensation some people spend their lives in search of—but I am happy when it passes and I can stand again. I pop the lights back on, walk back out the tunnel, and tell a smiling

but many of these original timber-sets are still in good shape, still functioning to support the tunnel. Most of the Country Boy is not timbered and this means that we have a good strong tunnel. We put timbers up only in spots that seem unstable. (*Some days you may feel like you should erect a couple of timber sets in your ribcage.*) The areas where you see lots of timber-sets are where we had to work through a cave-in to open up the tunnel. You may notice that most of the old timbers are slimy to the touch. When the mine inspector comes to the Country Boy, he walks the tunnel, stopping at each timber set. He always checks the old ones; and it's not with some kind of handheld computer device or other high-tech gauge. No, he just pulls out a screwdriver and jabs it in the timber. That's the test. It's that simple, that unscientific. He's just looking for rot. (*Some days you might think it's a good thing he doesn't jab you with a screwdriver.*)

Doug that I had a great time exploring and that I'll have to do it again real soon.

CAVE-INS

Before I worked at the Country Boy I didn't realize that cave-ins are sort of like car wrecks. There are degrees of harm and danger. They're not all catastrophic. Some cave-ins are the equivalent of a little fender-bender, maybe a minor pile-up. But some of them are much much worse.

One morning Betsy and I open the mine and turn on the air bag. We let Jumper and Whitey out of the pen and set some gold pans out. By the time the first tourists arrive, the sun has crept up over the divide and started to warm the thin mountain air. I line people up outside the portal and start into my tour guide spiel.

I'm feeling good, having fun. It's a good-sized group, probably nine or ten in all. We move through the first few stops on the tour in good shape and make our way down the tunnel to the stope. You will find many such stopes in old gold mines. Most of them were worked for a while and then abandoned as clay seams or other faults. These are also some of the most unstable places in the tunnel because the rock is softer and weaker.

As I find my usual mark, just below the viewing-gap, I notice a rock and dirt piled in between the tracks. I try not to make a point of it as I kick a couple of rocks aside and rest my foot on the pile as if it's always been there. I look up through the hole and notice that several other larger rocks have landed on the timber set, just above where the tourists are now standing. I talk quickly, cutting out several talking points, and hurry the group past the stope, down the tunnel, hoping the whole time that one of them doesn't get crushed by another falling rock and that the cave-in doesn't get worse and block our exit.

I finish the tour and, after a few anxious moments as we pass under the stope again, we all make it out of the tunnel in fine shape; but I track down Doug right away and tell him about the cave-in. While Betsy takes the group over to the gold panning creek, Doug and I grab two large steel rods and head back to the stope. We climb up on top of the timber-set and move the larger rocks aside.

Doug points at a large divot in the eight-by-eight timber, "Whew, look at that," he says. "Think what that would do to you."

Of course I'm already doing this, picturing a tourist's skull sheered off like a coconut husk and the meaty brain exposed to all this dust and dirt and wetness[8].

---

8   Stop Three: Boiler Room Script

(*Read verbatim or adapt to own style.*) This is the fun part. This is when I get to ask for a volunteer. How about you, son? Come on up here (*He may be shy at first but parents will push him into it.*) I'll need for you to take this small sledgehammer we keep there in the tunnel. I'll take this large steel spike and place it in a hole we've made here in the rocks.

Single-jacking is one miner working alone. So you pound the spike with the sledge. (*Ping. Ping. Ping.*) All alone.

You have to twist the steel to keep it from getting lodged in there. (*Ping. Ping. Ping.*) Toiling in this tunnel hour after hour. Pounding and twisting the steel. (*Ping. Ping.*) (*The boy may be getting tired at this point.*) It was primitive drilling. Just making a pattern of holes—eight hours a day, every day. And then filling those holes with dynamite.

I hope you're not too tired, because now I'll ask you to help me demonstrate double jacking. But I'll give you the easy job. Hold the steel for me, and I'll pick up this big sledgehammer. You twist and I'll swing. The two of us dancing. It's a team effort, like any relationship. But it's going to be loud. OK?

"OK," Doug says, "This is what we call 'barring down.' Basically the point is to knock the loose rock down so it doesn't fall like this," he points down at the pile on the tracks. "So we'll stand on opposite sides and kind of work the same spots. You'll see how it goes, but you can kind of guide the rock down with the bar."

At this point I must look terribly confused or frightened or both, because Doug says, "Don't worry, OK?"

"Sure."

"Watch."

Doug raises his bar up and I follow his lead. He

(Right now, the boy will be staring at you, trying to decide if he should trust you. His parents too. He might look up at you from beneath a baseball cap. He might remind you of yourself when you were younger and dreamed of living in the mountains. Yes, maybe he too is obsessed with My Side of the Mountain *and fantasizes about living in the burned-out stump of an old tree; but you will never know this for sure.)*

So with the pounding of the hammer and the noise of all the other miners, if you need me to stop swinging my sledge for any reason, the only way to signal me will be to do what the old miners did. OK? Are you with me?

If you want to get my attention, you'll need to place your thumb over the end of the steel spike. Like this. *(You say and slide your thumb slowly over the flattened end to demonstrate. Be dramatic about it. Raise your sledgehammer. He will pull his hand away and cower behind his parents. They will be laughing and cringing, they will imagine the big sledge meeting the tiny bones of the thumb, legions of thumbless men dropping beer mugs in bars because they can't grip it right.)*

("Yeawww!" the boy might say.)

Oh, don't worry. I've only crushed a couple of thumbs. *(People will laugh if you say this right.)* And just think. The Old Miners were working by candlelight. I bet there were more than a few missing thumbs.

Any other volunteers?

starts jabbing at the rock.

"You can hear the difference," he says, and he's right. The loose rock sounds hollow when you tap it. The hardrock is just hard.

Doug taps on a chunk of rock and I join him. Soon a roof-shingle-sized chunk comes loose and Doug sort of pins it to the wall and actually does *guide* it down.

"That's pretty fucking cool," I say.

"Yeah," Doug says, "I love this shit."

We keep working the stope together, knocking down small to large-sized chunks and sheets of rock. It's as if the stope is molting, shedding old skin. I get confident in my abilities and start working some spots on my own. I whack a chunk of rock and it breaks loose immediately. I try to guide it down, but it bounces and falls straight for Doug. He spots it just in time and deflects the chunk to the side with his bar. It slides down his bar for a second, then drops and smacks the timber set, leaving a divot twice the size of the one we'd admired on the way in.

"That was a close one," he says.

"Sorry."

"That's OK. Just be careful."

We keep working the stope, knocking loose a somewhat frightening amount of rock. It piles up on the timbers and we shovel it down the hole into an ore cart—much like the old miners might have done. We muck up the stuff left on the tracks and push the ore cart down the tunnel and out to the tailings dump Doug and I built, and that's it. Thirty minutes later, I lead another group of tourists down the tunnel and stand beneath the stope, telling them about those crazy Blast Monkeys[9].

                Boiler Bullets

After the turn of the century and the development of steam engine technology, the old miners used a drill they call the Widowmaker (*which of course is the standard name for any object or obstacle that kills legions of men*). It's basically a piston-driven hammer that pulverized the rock into fine razor dust, or hard-rock silica. It probably pulverized a foot bone or two, but that's not how the Widowmaker kills. Before the advent of "wet" drills that used a directed stream of water to control the dust, the old miners inhaled rock-dust, or silica, in large quantities. These tiny little razors cut into the pink tissue of their lungs, shredded them slowly and filled the lobes with rock-dust until they began to bleed and ooze fluid. Eventually the Old Miner drowned in his own blood.

We have a couple of the old Widowmakers (*Point at drills lodged in rock, abandoned mid-job*) set up for show and Doug has drilled out a sample pattern on one wall. (*Sometimes during a tour you might want to step up to the drill and pretend to jack a couple of holes. Sometimes Doug actually uses the drills, but the noise is almost unbearable so you might do it once and never again.*) In the photos of the Old Miners they're always posing with their tools. Take a look when we get back to the surface. It's never just a man. It's a man and his hammer, his steel, his helmet, his boots, his muscles (*his scars, his bleeding lungs*) and his Widowmaker drill cradled like a baby. (*Don't spend too much time staring at the pictures, trying to identify with the faces.*) The men do not smile but you get the sense this is not because they won't, but because they can't. They're just too tired and can't understand why someone is pointing a camera at them and interrupting their work.

The hydraulic drills ran off of a steam boiler. As you can see we still have the original Country Boy boiler. (*Point to boiler-tank huddled in the corner.*) It's approximately twelve feet long and five feet tall, tucked into this cove blasted out of the tunnel. As you can also see, they used rivets to construct this boiler—which worked pretty well most of the time. (*Finger rivets, the polished nubs of steel.*) But every now and then the Old Miners had to deal with a boiler explosion that turned lead rivets into bullets buzzing down the tunnels. I can almost hear them pinging off the rock walls. Can't you? This was just one of many things in the mine that took husbands from wives, fathers from children, boyfriends from girlfriends—just one

NOTES ON MUCK

Muck is what's left after eight hours of drilling and blasting out a pattern of holes. The Old Miners worked all day to make a pile of *muck*. It's all the rubble and mud left after a shift in the tunnel. *Mucking* is the action of shoveling *muck* into ore carts strapped to burros. If I were an Old Miner, if I was a miner at all and not a lonely tour guide, I'd spend the first few hours of my shift *mucking*. One of my first days there, Doug takes me back into the mine, down to the end of the main tunnel, past a roped off area where the *Mucker* is parked.

"If you're here in the winter," he says, "we'll do some *mucking*. We plan to open up more tunnels to tourists. You plan to be here in the winter, don't you?

"Yeah, sure. I can't wait for the snow."

"We'll be doing some serious mucking. We'll need you then," he says, placing his hand on my shoulder.

"Cool," I say because I don't know what else to say.

I feel like I should pledge my allegiance to him, agree to spend my days mucking the fuck out of the Country Boy's dark tunnels, but I just can't do it. Not yet, anyway. I really haven't given this place much of a chance, but I feel like I can't get a foothold. I haven't even seen the snow yet, haven't dug my truck out of

---

of any number of Widowmakers they faced in a day of work. (*This was real danger, real risk, real sacrifice. The old miners could teach you a thing or two about sacrifice.*)

a drift, or stomped through a forest in snowshoes. I haven't skied a day and I'm worried if I'll even make it to winter[10].

We'll pause here for a moment beneath the Stope. You can see that we've built new timber-sets here to support the tunnel. (*You may need to call your girlfriend when you get home tonight, just to feel like she supports you.*) This was the largest cave-in they found when the new owners first excavated the main tunnel of the Country Boy. We've left a hole for you to see the Stope. This is an area in the tunnel were the Old Miners, blasting their way into the mountain, found a soft spot in the rocks, a spot they believed might be a gold-producing vein. (*It's always the soft spots. That's where you feel this emptiness sometimes, noisy like a moth fluttering around in a light fixture.*)

It may come as a surprise that the Old Miners would work up into a vein. (*Try to suppress any images of blood-filled veins and hearts pumping.*) I for one always assumed that you dug down into a vein and mined out what was inside—just like I always assumed that mine tunnels would go down into a mountain. Anyone else think the same thing? (*Look for a show of hands. Note those who admit to thinking the same. Make eye contact. These are your friends. These are your big-tippers.*) But of course it makes sense that they would use gravity to their advantage. The Old Miners were no dummies. (*You may not be able to say the same for yourself.*)

If you look up into the Stope you'll see that we've placed some dummies up there on ladders and scaffolding. (*Wait to see if anyone gets your joke.*) They're pretending to be Old Miners, jacking holes in the rock, getting ready for the Blast Monkey. Now I'll need another volunteer. (*Look for another kid, one hiding in the back.*) You there, the shy one. I need a Blast Monkey. (*Bring the kid to the front. Hand her a stick of dynamite you keep stashed nearby.*) Ok now your job will be to climb up into the Stope after they've drilled their holes. This is typically done at the end of the day. You would climb up in there and fill the holes with dynamite. You'd light all the fuses, scamper back down the ladder, and scream, "Fire in the hole." Can you do that?

"Fire in the holes!!" the girl yells.

And then you'd have to run out of the mine as fast as you can. The Blast Monkey is always the last one out of the Mine. So what do you think? Are you ready to be our Blast Monkey? (*The kid will*

Doug ducks under the chain and I follow him. Standing in front of the *Mucker*, he tells me that the advent of steam technology spawned the creation of steam-powered *muckers*—large tractor-like mining machines that roll on the narrow gauge tracks and do the mucking work of several men.

"This one runs on the air compressor."

The Country Boy has a large air compressor that powers most of the mining tools these days. It's much more efficient and much safer than steam.

The Mucker is a hulking yellow and black machine covered with dirt and grease. The paint is chipped and battered. It looks like an armored troll, huddled in the tunnel. Equipped with a lifting shovel on the front that scoops and dumps, the Mucker pulls an ore-cart behind and fills it as it moves. It's basically an automated shovel-and-bucket operation. Nothing fancy. But maybe it's the dim light or just my crazy brain, but I get the feeling that this machine has a history, a personality. It looks like if you pissed it off, it would disengage one of its shovel arms, club you over the head, and bury your corpse in a pile of muck.

As much as I like saying "muck," I try to avoid thinking too much about rubble and wreckage—because *muck* may be all that's left of my relationship when I'm done here. But this is not the kind of metaphorical connection I want to share with tourists or with Doug. He doesn't want to know. And the tourists haven't come to the Country Boy for this. They've come to hear about

shake her head. Take the dynamite back and hide it away. Move the group past the Stope, encourage them to look up. Try not to think about your day up there with Doug and the rocks dropping like shingles.)

the hardy Old Miners, Tommyknockers[11], cute little burros pulling ore carts[12], Red Light Districts, and non-

(*Stop beneath a moldy timber set, just past the boiler, where the tunnel gets dark again.*) Perhaps you've heard about the ghostly tapping of Tommyknockers—those apparitions of Old Miners haunting the tunnels? If everyone will fall silent and pay close attention, listen . . . Do you hear it? *Tap. Tap. Tap.* (*Wait long enough and the sound will come.*) There's a ghost trapped in the tunnel, buried by a cave-in. He's a Tommyknocker tapping to get out. (*It's true. You can always hear a faint tapping—sort of like Poe's telltale heart. But this isn't a reference that will get you a lot of tips. The noise is probably just the drip-drip of water.*) If we sat long enough listening in the dark we'd probably hear more than we want. Sensory deprivation does that to you. We have the benefit of electric lights, but I can't help but think about what all that darkness would've done to the mind of an Old Miner. Miners are a superstitious lot. Something about working 8 hours a day beneath thousands of tons of rock, constantly at the mercy of fate, makes you arm yourself with superstitions and magical incantations. Whistling in the tunnel is a big no-no, the kind of thing that might have got you a beating in the old days. The old miners believed the sound was some kind of affront to the mountain, a laugh in the face of chance, and if I ever slip up and let out a whistle, you be sure to remind me of my mistake. (*The truth is you will have no interest in tempting fate and very rarely whistle while I work. The mountain is powerful big and magical; and sometimes I swear there's a Tommyknocker tapping in my chest. If I listen close, my lonely underground heart sounds like a hammer hitting rock. There's nothing muscular, nothing human about it.*) I will, of course do the same if one of you should happen to let a whistle slip. (*Point to a particularly happy kid, give him a stern look, as if to say "I'm watching you."*) Of course this also means that the Seven Dwarves of Snow White fame would have been committing some serious violations of tunnel protocol by "whistling while they work." (*Pause for laughter.*)

You may have noticed Jumper, our miniature burro. (*Pause for moment of recognition.*) Many mines in the old days used burros to pull their ore carts around the tunnels. The animals were born in the mine, spent their whole lives there, and were typically rendered

threatening hookers in pantaloons.

blind from all the darkness—their eyes atrophying over time—
and deaf from all the noise. (*Don't wait for the gasp, the sympathetic
moan, because this is the sad part of the tour, the part you don't sugarcoat.*)
Sometimes when the burros grew too old to work they were taken
to the surface and, all too often, the light and air and wind shocked
and panicked them so much they simply jumped back down the
shaft. They probably just wanted to go home.

MEET ME ALL THE WAY

For Labor Day weekend, my girlfriend and I decide to meet halfway between Breck and Lawrence in the small town of Oakley, Kansas[13]. It's about a six-hour drive each way, a compromise of sorts. We haven't seen each other for over a month now and our phone conversations seem to get more and more strained. There's a distance in the sound of her voice that frightens me—a distance not related to telephone technology or miles between us. I tell myself that she's protecting herself from getting hurt, but part of me realizes that she is also flat pissed off at me for abandoning her. I can't really blame her. I don't really know what I would have done if the situation had been reversed and she was the one who had left me.

Oakley is a mile or so off of I-70, and the Kansas Kountry Inn is the first motel you find when you drive into town. For the entire trip, I've been going over in my head all the things I want to say to her, all the stories I want to tell her about living in the mountains. I've been telling myself to focus on the positive, on the moment,

---

13   A Light in the Tunnel

You folks may have noticed our electric lights in the tunnel. (*Point to string of lights running along the tracks.*) Even with these, you see how dark the tunnel can be. Light just sort of disappears. Well we're spoiled compared to the Old Miners (*remove white stub of a candle from your coveralls*) who often only had one candle between two of them. One tiny candle to light their work; and these candles were valuable commodities that were rationed by the mining companies. (*Hold up candle for them to inspect.*) You can be sure there were times when the men were working mostly in the dark, more by feel than by sight.

and not worry about the future.

When I pull into the parking lot, I see my girlfriend's white Toyota Camry parked in front of a room near the vending machines. My heart pings and shudders. I pull in next to her car and see the window curtains part slightly, then drop back into place. As I climb out of my pickup, the door swings open and she runs out. She literally jumps into my arms, wraps her legs around my waist, and I squeeze her tight, kissing her hard and deep and long. I try to speak, but my voice catches. I can barely make a sound.

We talk rapidly in quick bursts of words, spilling out details from our daily lives—the little things we've missed; and then we just hold each other for a while, saying nothing.

We eat that night at Shirley's Restaurant in downtown Oakley and it's quite clear that we're the only non-resident patrons. But we don't care. We eat our salty, gravy-laden food and love every bite, convinced it's the best meal we've had in over a month. The next day we take a road trip to the Chalk Pyramids, a formation of chalky outcroppings that do indeed rise up out of the prairie like ancient temples. The entire area is rich with fossilized marine life and undersea vegetation. We're the only humans around for miles, but for the first time in a long time, I don't feel alone.

We stay at the Kansas Kountry Inn for two days, emerging from our air-conditioned room occasionally for food and drink, and then it happens; we have to say goodbye all over again. We've tried not to talk about it, tried to just focus on the present, but I'm unprepared when the time of goodbyes approaches like a storm and slams into us. We move toward each other, mash, sob, and push away; stumble to cars, fall inside, sink, whimper, and fade.

As I steer out of the parking lot of the Kansas Kountry Inn, cross the Interstate to head west and watch my girlfriend take the exit for I-70 East, I feel part of myself accelerate away from me, merge with traffic, and disappear into the shimmering heat.

SALTING THE EARTH

At the Country Boy you're guaranteed to strike gold. We make sure of it. All you have to do is spend a little time panning down by the stream. If you're careful, you can't miss. Doug buys gold flakes by the ounce and, at the end of the day, I sprinkle 2 or 3 flakes in each pan and cover them with dirt. After every tour, I give each guest their own pan filled with dirt "taken out of the mine" and then I show them how to work the pan and swirl the water around, separating out the dirt and rocks until there's fine black silt and a sparkle of gold.

The kids especially love gold panning and get very excited when they find their gold. They often need a place to put their treasure and I happen to carry small glass vials in my coveralls that they can purchase for 75 cents. It doesn't matter what I say on the tour, how many stories I tell or jokes I make. If they find gold in their pan we know they're coming back. We know that's what they'll remember from their visit and what they'll show off to friends. It's good for public relations. One flake of gold, one nugget of value makes it all meaningful. Sure it's a bit of a deception, but the lie makes people so happy. Just a little white lie allows them to believe in the dream. What's so wrong with that? [14]

---

14   Last Stop: Right Fork

(*This is it.*) If I can get everyone to follow me down the right fork of the tunnel, we have one last stop on the tour. If you can please walk all the way up to the rope, I'll stop here in the middle where everyone can hear me. (*You may have to coach them on movement. They'll be inclined to mill around and hesitant to move forward without your lead.*) Now if you take a look down this fork of the tunnel you can get an idea of what this main tunnel looked like when we first excavated the Country Boy. Lots of muck and water and crumbling timber-sets. (*Point to collapsed timbers.*) But there are also timber-sets still in good shape. You'll also notice the piles and piles of rock that will have to be mucked out of the tunnel. We hope to start working on this tunnel sometime during the winter months, when things slow down a bit. Now up to this point we've had the luxury of our electric lights; but I thought I'd give you folks an idea of how dark it actually gets in the mine. So if everyone's ready, I'll go ahead and pop off the lights for a few seconds. (*This is when you hit the switch and drop everyone into darkness. This is when you have the urge to flee. The dark is immediate and overwhelming for some people. It's not the kind of dark you're accustomed to. It's darkness without the possibility of light. No reprieve. No forgiveness.*) As you folks can see, it gets quite dark in the tunnel without electric or battery powered light. Remember the Old Miners only had one candle for every two to three of them. Listen up. Quiet, please. You can hear the trickle of water. Any Tommyknockers out there? (*This is when you strike the match and give them a flicker of light. This is when you light the candle. This is when you hope that your girlfriend is more forgiving than the dark.*) Now you can imagine how difficult it would be to work those hammers and drills, how hard it would be to see that thumb-signal from your partner to stop swinging his sledgehammer. (*Sometimes at the end of the day, when the air back here is getting thin, you may have trouble lighting the candle. It may just be a dying flicker, the kind of thing that doesn't inspire much confidence in you as a tour guide, a bringer of light and knowledge.*) I'll flip on the lights and hang out back at the cave-in to answer any questions you might have. Feel free to take photos and join me on the surface for some gold panning in our stream.

Because of my mild claustrophobia, cramped spaces or crowds cause my pulse to race and I get very anxious. I begin to sweat and fidget. I have to suppress the urge to flee. But surprisingly I don't feel this way in the Country Boy's tunnels; and this worries me a little. I don't want to get too used to being alone. I realize that now, perhaps when it's too late.

I think part of the reason my anxiety doesn't burn and spike when I'm in the mine is because I'm in control. I'm the tour guide. I'm the boss, the one with all the information. I know the way in and out of this hole. I know everyone will follow me.

My apartment, however, seems like a natural extension of my roommate Kent—often more cave-like and reminiscent of a mine-tunnel than an actual mine-tunnel. It's dark, musty, and smells funky like old wet shoes. It's on the ground level of a four-story concrete-block building and the ceilings seem to sag with the weight of all the other tenants above us. The walls are paneled with walnut-veneer paneling. One of them is draped with a thick purple velour curtain and our couch is covered with orange velour.

To be honest, it looks like a set from a David Lynch film—the kind of place where you might find a severed ear in a potted plant. The apartment, even empty, feels vaguely malevolent. Our kitchen has two pans, three bowls, four plates, and a few bits of mismatched silverware. In one bedroom, Rob has built a sleeping-loft out of lodge-pole pines. With the bark still on the logs, it resembles a funeral pyre. I have a Thermo-rest pad on the floor below with a sleeping bag and a blue plastic milk-crate for a nightstand. Neither one of us wants to share a room with Kent, but one day we lose electricity in half the room and discover evidence of a small fire in the closet. It's not a place where sleep comes easily and stays with you all night.

One morning after I had a particularly rough night full of anxiety dreams and sleeplessness, I'm sitting on the couch writing in my journal when Kent comes out of his room. He's wearing boxer shorts and nothing else. His hairy belly hangs over the waistband. He's rubbing his chest and looks battered, greasy, and troll-like—sort of like the *Mucker* at the Country Boy.

"Chest hurts," he says, pinching up his face.

"You having chest pains?" I ask, wondering if his diet has exacted some kind of revenge on his body.

"No," he says, "Burned it."

"Huh?"

Kent tells me how he's been smoking dope in bed this morning. Apparently he was tapping out the pipe on his chest because he didn't want to get up and use an ashtray. So he tapped out a burning ember, singing chest hair, and leaving a tiny red welt next to his left nipple. Kent steps closer to me, showing me his trophy spot.

"Hurts," he says, turning and lurching back to the bathroom.

I thought this was all I ever wanted—life with my buddies, free and happy, unencumbered by girlfriends or commitments. Lots of beer and dope and camping in the woods. Lots of snowboarding adventures. But instead I feel buried beneath the weight of loneliness, trapped behind a cave-in. I find myself welling up with tears at inappropriate moments. I can barely participate in the usual rituals of drinking, smoking, and bullshitting; and it's later that day, when Kent has gone off to work, that I sit down on the orange couch next to Rob, my oldest and dearest friend.

"I don't think I can make it," I say, "I'm just not happy."

"You're not having fun?" "Nope," I say, "not really. I've tried but I just can't get past this," and I want to be more specific, more rational and calm, but I start bawling and can't stop. The look on his face tells me he's disappointed, but Rob says that he understands. He probably does. There's maybe nobody on the planet who understands me better than he does. I tell him I'll stick it out until October. Doug needs me at the mine until then, but I suggest that he and Kent try to find another place to live.

The Old Miners lived to an average age of 42 years. Many of them died from breathing huge quantities of rock dust created by the first "Widowmaker" drills. Eventually they'd drown to death, suffocated by their own body. These men lived and breathed these mountains until they couldn't breathe any longer. They died young for their dreams of riches, fame, and independence[15].

I don't want to be a pioneer. It's been done before in much better form. Instead I want to blaze a trail back home, a path of return to my girlfriend, because it now seems more adventurous, more brave, than running for the hills at the first wink of commitment, and I'm tired of suffocating. I want to breathe again.

---

15   A Final Note for Tour Guides

(*Of course it's natural for you to fall for the promise of independence, that idealized vision of the mountains and the West that rewards strapping young men for their independence. You grew up in Kansas. You want to be like that boy in* My Side of the Mountain. *We know this. It's natural for you to ignore the Old Miners—their pain, their lungs full of fluid. It's natural for you to want to carve some identity from the Country Boy, and there's room for that here. But you know it's not an easy job. You know that happiness is not hardrock, not that tangible. Perhaps, like silence or love, it's only something you acutely appreciate after it's gone. But we still expect you to pull your rubber boots on every day and trudge into the tunnel, telling the stories, mining the tourists, at least for another month or two.* If you can't grow it, you have to mine it. *It's only now that you know the hole by heart when you will make the decision to return to her, the choice of sweet dependence. It's only now, at the end, that you no longer need a guidebook.*

Good luck, son.)

36

Next Stop,
Meteor Crater

APARTMENT SINGLE

This is where we are—settled now in Flagstaff, Arizona. The high desert. And at night the skunks come down out of the pine forest to eat seed dropped by the chickadees and finches that frequent our feeder. The skunks circle patios, lick barbecue drippings, and taunt the locked-up dogs in the apartments below. I'm glad our place is on the second floor and we don't have to hear them snickering in the grass outside our windows. Instead I stand on our balcony at night, nursing the stub of a joint, and stare down at their squirming backs. I toss sunflower seeds, hoping to hit them, and I hiss like a tomcat—trying to provoke them into spraying the neighbors' windows.

It's like this here.

BIG OL' COUNTRY MONDAY

I-40 early morning. Commuting to Meteor Crater, and it's just us and the truckers. Fools of a different feather. Carlos, the forty-five year-old recovering addict, sits cross-legged in the back seat of our Toyota. His eyes are closed. He is mentally preparing himself for a day of work at the Meteor Crater Snackbar. This morning I have sewage trap duty and my girlfriend works in the Rock Shop cracking geodes. Later we'll get to guide some tours on the rim. Carlos will stay in the snackbar all day. Carlos loves the snackbar.

The sun has barely split the horizon and I'm already thinking about the end of the day, the drive home, and the squirming skunks coming down from the woods. On NPR Nina Totenberg talks about a recent Supreme Court decision. The morning highway rolls out naked and whiskered with frost. Carlos recites his poem, *Pocket Watch. Tick, tock. Tick, tock.* When will he shut the fuck up? Slowly, I twist the volume knob until Nina's voice crackles with static and my speakers fuzz. Backseat drivers are one thing. Backseat poets are something else.

This must be the fourth time in two weeks I've heard *Pocket Watch.* Carlos keeps adding stanzas and removing lines. *Pocket Watch, Pocket Watch, how does your garden grow?* But I can't decide which is worse, the imposition of bad poetry or his detailed stories of wild times in Long Beach, including passing mention of anal sex with Freddy Krueger and coke parties with soap opera stars. I don't ask him to elaborate. He does anyway.

Carlos moved out here to shake his methamphetamine habit. Now he lives with his thirty-five year-old nephew's family, and commutes to work with us. He doesn't have a car of his own, but he's thinking about buying a moped. Once we invited him to our house for dinner after work and he wasn't there ten minutes before he had his shirt off and was dancing around our living room in a frenzied form of what he called "relaxation exercises"—something that looked more like a bizarre mating ritual of South American waterfowl. This is just one of the times that I've asked myself the nagging question, "What the hell are we doing here?"

THE BEST AND THE WORST

The best mornings have me standing on the rim of Meteor Crater, watching the sun creep up in the east and spread color out over the high desert like orange paste. To the west, the San Francisco Peaks rise 12,000 feet over Flagstaff, purple as eggplant and adorned with skirts of tangerine clouds. The snowy-white floor of the crater, almost 600 feet below, is still dark in the indigo shadows—the old mining equipment, the upturned lip of the south side, and the white band of Coconino sandstone that rings the entire circumference. I see large chunks of rock, the rubble from the impact, spread out around the crater and I imagine the waves of devastation rippling out from this very center, rolling up to the purple peaks in the distance, falling into Walnut Canyon, slipping over the Mogollon rim.

The best mornings have me outside, under the big desert sky, inevitably alone, walking the trail, embracing this place of apocalyptic past. The tourists have just begun to trickle in from the highway. My girlfriend is working inside, readying the Rock Shop or the Gift Shop for their arrival. Carlos is prepping the snackbar, heating the nacho cheese sauce. The day has barely begun but still seems full of promise, possibility, even new challenges.

The worst mornings have me holding a long wooden pole affixed with a wire hanger, breathing through my mouth.

The worst mornings have me fishing waterlogged tampons out of the Meteor Crater sewage trap and dropping them in a galvanized aluminum trashcan. There's no denying it. They look like headless rats, their tails hanging off the wire and writhing in the air. They hit the bottom of the trash can with a lewd wet slap.

The worst mornings have me thinking that we haven't escaped anything here, but fallen smack dab in the middle of another hole in the ground.

POSTCARD

The laser-enhanced sky is bright laser-enhanced blue and the crater looks something like a giant wound in the desert; or a cigarette burn on old flesh, a puncture wound, a cattle brand; maybe a melanoma blossoming on sun-stretched skin.

Black asphalt parking lots, red-brick buildings—low slung like rest-stop architecture, and just a rocky ridge that lifts up from the flat plain. Izzy and Putter are there to meet you. They are married and retired. Entirely. They live together in a RV and work the ticket windows. They listen to twangy country music all day long and talk at tourists through an inch of bullet-resistant Plexiglas. They eat sack lunches and take walks together. They are deeply and profoundly happy.

It is at the Ticket Window, after a six-mile drive from I-40, that tourists discover the cost of admission: $8 per person. And they might point at the beige uniforms, the brown *Natural Landmark* signs, stammering something about their expectations for a *National Park*, for Smokey the Bear, for the park-standard $10 per car entrance fee. But it's no use. They've driven all this way. The parking lot, the road, the crater itself–everything is surrounded by chain-link fence. They find themselves at the front of a line, no way to go back easily, no "chicken" exits like they used to have on the roller coasters back home. You can say whatever you want, but Izzy and Putter have heard it all before.

Behind them tumbleweeds skitter through the parking lot.

A massive crow perched on the blue trashcan squawks loudly and seems to stare hungrily at their children.

This is when they have to make a decision: pay the eight dollars per person or drive the six miles back to I-40 and try to forget this detour. But Putter knows what to say to ease your mind. He tells you proudly that this Meteor Crater is privately owned and operated independent of the government, free of any government shutdowns that locked the gates of several *other* attractions in this area.

That's right. Someone *owns* a geological phenomenon. To be more precise, a massive cattle ranching operation called B&B owns the largest impact crater in North America. Putter assures you that you are in good hands. But this doesn't really make you feel any better as you hand your ticket over and push through the turnstile.

TEST QUESTION

Did the impact occur before or after Jesus was born?[1]
   a.   After.
   b.   Day 5 of creation.
   c.   Maybe Day 6 (it's hard to be sure).
   d.   50,000 years ago.
   e.   None of the above.

---

1 And this is another one of those questions that forces me to halt the spiel and engage my brain—not so much in an attempt to answer the question reasonably, but in an effort to answer it without offending the questioner. Most of the time, this doesn't work and I end up answering "D," I'll say, "The meteor hit fifty thousand years ago," and then wait for them to say something else before I say again, "Fifty thousand years, " and then if they still don't get it, "Jesus was born roughly two thousand years ago." I don't really know how else to answer this question. I usually feel like I'm failing some sort of test. This question often comes after I've dated rock layers at 250 million years, as if they're testing whether I'll stick to my facts.

SCALE

Try to imagine twenty football games being played simultaneously on the floor of the crater, the mother of all Bowl Games[2] with one million fans watching from the sides of the crater. Five hundred fifty feet is about a fifty-five-story building. Imagine the Statue of Liberty standing on the floor, staring you in the eye, the points of her crown just peeking over the rim. From I-40 the crater looks like any other butte or small mesa. The rim has been eroded over time by fierce winds and rain. But the view down from the rim is something special. You can see so many stories spelled out in the rocks—creation, destruction, hubris and angst. See that boiler tank on the bottom of the crater, a remnant from Barringer's mining days.[3] That boiler tank is the size of a school bus.[4]

---

2 Wink knowingly at the sun-pinked tourist with his Dallas Cowboys cap.

3 Point to the boiler tank and hold your thumb and forefinger up, framing the tank between them.

4 That boiler tank is the size of a mini-van. That boiler tank is the size of a mobile home. That boiler tank fits between your thumb and forefinger.

POSTCARD

Jackalope hops over Saguaro cacti. Big as a Kangaroo
with antlers sprouting from his skull. The poor
marginalized beast. Not quite bunny. Not quite ungulate.

STUPID QUESTION

Do jackalopes really exist?

STUPID ANSWER

Yes. They're nocturnal and highly aggressive. If you bait a trap with peanut butter and raw chicken, you're sure to catch one.[5]

---

5 After doing this for a while, I just start saying what people want to hear. But I never specify what kind of trap to use. That would be too easy.

PROFESSIONAL STANDARDS

Management passed a rule after we started working: No reading on the clock unless it is a book you purchase from the Gift Shop.

There isn't one other person in the whole place who has a remote interest in reading at work. They just smoke and swap stories about steak-houses and smorgasbords. We're there for ten-hour shifts. If we're lucky we give four tours a day. The rest of the time, we were stuck behind the retail counter. We get twenty minutes for lunch. And the only other breaks are smoke breaks—something that has actually caused me to entertain the idea of taking up smoking, or at least pretending to smoke. But it's October now. Wind rips across the desert and nobody ever comes to see the Crater anymore. Most of my tours average two or three people. Some days it's eight hours sitting behind a retail counter listening to the new age CD's play incessantly—the whisper of whales, the lullaby of the lemurs, the chortle of sea turtles. It's enough to make anyone homicidal.

Banned from reading anything besides Cowboy Cookbooks and Ghost Stories of the Ol' West, I start writing in my journal—feverishly sometimes—and I think it frightens my coworkers. I can tell they want to make another rule about writing at work, but they're probably afraid of singling me out too much. Sometimes they ask me what I'm writing about; and it rarely goes well. Often I'll just say, "I'm writing about you," and this is usually enough to silence them. One day behind the Gift Shop counter, Kenny asks the question.

"You really want to know?" I ask.

"Sure," he says, "Is it about me?"

"No. Not today," I say. "I'm outlining some

arguments for active euthanasia."

"For what?"

"Euthanasia. You know, it's sort of like physician assisted killing, like if someone is brain dead, just being kept alive by a respirator."

"Oh, you mean like Jack Kevorkian."

I didn't have the heart or patience to explain how far active euthanasia is from Kevorkian's VW van of death, so I just said, "Yeah, that's pretty much it."

"Cool," he says.

I just keep on writing, probably more feverishly than before. Everything makes it to those pages. All the gory details . . . Our engagement earlier this summer in Costa Rica. Our first time living away from home—though we'd traveled extensively. Living in a cookie-cutter apartment complex with a kitchen the size of most closets. One apartment looked just like the next—numbers the only thing that distinguishes one from the other. And the job seemed romantic at first. Meteor Crater. Tour Guide. Hired storyteller. But they never mentioned the sewage trap, the long wooden pole and the waterlogged tampons looking like drowned rats.

They never mentioned Norm, the cowboy from upstate New York who, when he can't smoke indoors, picks his scabs and eats them; or Buck the Air Force vet who hates Bill Clinton so much it hurts and his surly wife Clara, who, despite having lost one breast to cancer, sucks down Virginia Slim cigarettes like someone's going to take them away from her. In the interview there was no word about Ron, who looks something like a pygmy John Denver and combs the desert for pot shards on the weekends bragging about clandestine missions into protected areas. What about Walter and his stumps for fingers? He seems to hate everyone; and he's the senior tour guide, our point man for interactions with the public. I keep thinking we're going to find something else here, some hidden vein of good we can tap into. But Kenny, the former fireman, won't stop talking about the tubule pregnancy his girlfriend had. He wants to gloat about drinking beer and balling Indian chicks in his pickup. Sam the ticket guy raises pigeons in Winslow and he's never seen the Grand Canyon. Walter keeps scratching his nose with his stumps. Carlos won't stop reciting *Pocket Watch. Tick tock. Tick tock.* Minutes grind by like hours. Weeks feel like months. Time warps and bogs around us.

OBVIOUS QUESTION

Is it time to move on?

MY GIRLFRIEND'S ANSWER

I think so.[6]

---

6 Is she just saying what we both want to hear?

COUPLEDOM

Ron's wife, Trina, is big and round and loud. She collects mail-order plates and mass-produced Kachina dolls. They live, like the other married couples, in housing provided by Meteor Crater. Their apartments are perched on the eastern edge of the crater, connected to the visitor center, and look out toward Winslow. They live next door to Kenny and Stacey, who married on Halloween night so they could move into the crater housing. Three other couples live in apartments—Buck and Clara, Carl and Janna, Louise and Stanley. Most of the rest park their RV's at the Meteor Crater RV Camp down by the Interstate. It's this whole strange subculture of semi-retired couples and more than once I've had bone-chilling thoughts that we might have stumbled into some desert-dwelling swingers club where the real fun happens after the tourists and townies leave. This of course isn't true. But I do try to imagine rich lives for most of these people, something else beyond the day-to-day grind of gift shop banter and bad cafeteria food. We are easily the youngest people working here and we stick out like co-eds in a bingo parlor. I can't help but worry that we'll end up here someday down the road– bored to death with retirement or broke as a joke, and working just to pass the time until we die, or working just to earn free hook-up privileges at the RV park.

BEACH BOY GENIUS

David doesn't belong here either. He's a bit of a trespasser too. His life outside the crater extends beyond flea markets and smorgasbords, beyond gun shows and antique shops. David is a townie too—along with me, my girlfriend and Carlos. He has a MFA in sculpture, owns horses and a beautiful 66 Dodge Shelby. He participates in Civil War re-enactments and is completely obsessed with the legacy of the Beach Boys, more specifically with the genius of Brian Wilson.

I love working with David because he keeps me entertained for hours talking about the pop revolution inspired by Brian Wilson, the magic of his musical ability combined with his increasingly eccentric, even insane personality. David was there on the Southern Cal beaches, riding a long board before the war in Vietnam.

He tells stories that make me want to love the Beach Boys—a band I had seen perform at an amusement park amphitheater without Brian Wilson or any sense of shame about milking their legacy for all the nostalgia dollars they could. He makes me really want to appreciate their influence on pop music. David can also recite details about Civil War battles, horror stories from the Andersonville prison camp; but he never talks about Vietnam. He was even an extra in the Denzel Washington movie, *Glory*. And I respect him for this, for all of this. I respect anyone with passions, pain, dreams, obsessions–anyone with a Big Life. David is the one person I see as a friend here. And he admits that, if it weren't for my girlfriend and me, he would have quit a long time ago.

SOUVENIRS

Chunk of petrified wood with fuzzy squirrel glued to it, scorpion encased in Lucite, cactus candy, geodes guaranteed to be hollow, polished stones stained blue and pink, Kachina dolls, hats, shirts, visors, tiny bits of meteorite, postcards and *authentic* Indian jewelry.

ATTENTION, PLEASE

Barringer wasn't the only one fascinated by the otherworldly quality of the crater. When NASA went looking for a place to train Apollo astronauts for their moon missions in the 60's and 70's, they came to Meteor Crater.[7] The astronauts lived and trained at the crater, driving their moon buggy up and down the rocky walls. They stomped around in the dusty floor, ankle deep in white Coconino powder. They climbed the walls in their moon suits.[8] The astronauts relaxed here on the rim too. If you look behind you,[9] you'll see a small bunker built into the hillside. Originally this was probably used to store dynamite and other mining supplies. Today we've used it to display some beer cans left by the Apollo astronauts. That's right, Coors beer was crucial to their training. Feel free to take a look at the astronaut's beer cans, but keep an eye out for rattlesnakes. They sometimes like to curl up in the shade there.[10]

---

7 And it's true—there are times when you stand on the crater rim, just as the sun is rolling up over the horizon and believe that you could bound across the lunar surface all the way home.

8 Gesture with open hand at walls, as if you are showing a car.

9 Point over their heads, watch them twist.

10 Wait for the man in the hat to step close, then make a soft rattling sound by fluttering your tongue against the roof of your mouth. Watch him jump. Laugh sympathetically. Hold your hands up, palms out, in a show of submission. Allow the tourists to take your picture. Pose with the antique beer cans. Pose with the family and pretend to drink from Neil Armstrong's beer can.

STARMAN

When Jeff Bridges dropped from the movie sky and fell
in love, I knew nothing of Meteor Crater. But you may
remember that Hollywood image of him scrambling
down a rocky slope into the bowl of Meteor Crater—
government helicopters and soldiers chasing him, their
thwop-thwopping blades thundering in the Crater
bowl. Starman, an alien trespasser was coming here to
go home. Meteor Crater was homebase for him, safe
territory. It was a rendezvous, an easy-to-spot target.
Looking at this place, perhaps you can understand
this, how it might seem like a portal to other worlds,
something alien ships would recognize and return to
visit.[11] The Starman's path slices a diagonal across the
northwestern wall of the crater, cutting just beneath
the large sandstone outcropping where we finish the
tour. It's a rocky hardscrabble path that's barely used
any longer, but it's a persistent reminder of the human
presence here, a mark of our restless and curious feet.
Many people ask if we will be going down in the crater,
and it pains me sometimes to tell them no. It pains me
because I feel the urge too, the compulsion to drop over
the edge and descend completely into the crater.

---

11 Point at the narrow rocky path that cuts across one wall. See
the tourists nod their heads in recognition. They like the idea
that aliens are connected to the crater somehow—even if it's a
fictional connection. You may like this too, the way it seems to say
something about your own predicament, but you probably don't
want to share that with the tourists.

END OF THE LINE[1]

If you look down on the right side of the crater you'll see something shining in the sun.[2] You're not the first people to be curious about Meteor Crater. In 1965 two amateur pilots flew their Cessna into the bowl of the crater, taking a few swings around, but couldn't get back out. Wind whipping across the desert blows up the rim and over the top, capping the crater with an invisible lid. They were trapped here too. The pilots tried and tried to push their plane through the wind but were finally slammed to the dusty floor. Both men survived but they wouldn't soon forget their visit to Meteor Crater. Still today visitors flock to the Crater—though most of them find it much easier to leave.[3]

Well, that's the end of the tour and I want to thank you all for coming today. I hope you enjoy the rest of your visit to Meteor Crater. Please let me know if you have any questions.[4]

---

1 Step out on the edge. The sandstone cliff is red and dusty beneath your feet. Sometimes the tourists will swoon.
2 Point at shiny object, say things like "There, just beneath that big rock.
3 Wait for laughter.
4 Stay there on the edge for a moment. Gaze down into the crater. Suppress that urge to jump. You feel a twinge of fear every now and then. But it's not the height that scares you. It's that sudden urge to jump, that momentary desire to fly, to escape.

MISNOMER

Meteor is wrong really. It's only a meteor when it's falling through our atmosphere, when it's in motion. Before that, call it a *meteroid* in orbit. Only when it hits the earth, does it become a *meteorite*. It's the *–ite* that suggests stagnancy or roots—as if it can no longer be separated from what is earth. Would a *humanite* then be the crash landing of a *humanoid*? Our life on earth lived between dirt and sky. We've stepped out of our orbits, and we no longer roam like *meteors*. My girlfriend and I have run from home and settled here as *humanites,* working at *Meteor* Crater, a giant hole in the ground.

ROOTS

We yanked them up and ran from Kansas. Landed on this lunar surface—unprepared for the change in gravity. Unlike the moon, we can't bounce so easy here. We feel anchored, stuck. But Kansas isn't what we want either— not any longer. The mountains of Colorado have begun to call again; and they sound a lot like my friend Rob saying, "Nine dollars an hour. Snowboarding every day. The mountains, the snow, the fun, the lack of sewage traps." The elevation also sounds nice—mountains popped up through the Earth's crush like inverted craters, the opposite of this place. Tourists like to ask where we're from. Though it's tempting to lie, we usually admit to migrating from Kansas. And still, people like to make the obligatory Wizard of Oz jokes—after all these years, after all the clichés. And it's hard for me to hide my disdain for their lack of creativity. "Well, you're not in Kansas anymore," they say. "Ha. Ha," I say. "That's funny." And I suppose it is sort of funny—not the joke, but the situation.[5] We aren't in Kansas anymore, Toto. We aren't anywhere familiar or safe. And I think this is what's missing—familiarity. Not necessarily family, but the roots of it. Connections. Some sense of security as we head down a new path toward marriage. We've made some friends here; but it always seemed more a matter of necessity than choice. When we listened to the calls from friends in Colorado, tempting us with their happiness, the ideas began to roll around in our heads.

5 See my brown pants, my shirt with the patches. See the crater hole in the massive sandstone shelf of the Colorado Plateau, this flat plain of our lives.

THREE-DAY WEEKEND

Most weekends we'd spend one day walking through one of the many parks and preserves. Strolling past cliff dwellings and lava tubes, gazing off the Mogollon rim, hiking in the San Francisco Peaks, visiting the Grand Canyon, listening to other tour guides—the two of us often wandering in silence. We don't ask questions. We don't interrupt the spiel.[6] Other days we make efforts to spend time alone, away from each other. We take solitary bike rides through the forest, departing in opposite directions. I sit alone on the porch with a book or my laptop computer. We have our loud fights, sure. But we seem to be getting along fine most of the time. We're just two very independent people who need their own passions and pursuits, their own time and space—and we've been crammed together by this job, this life of work[7]. On some level, it's hard for me to accept that we aren't happy in our barren cookie-cutter apartment or our jobs. It feels like a failure of nerve, a lack of adventurous spirit. We've traveled together many times, spending fifty days living out of my truck and tent one summer in Alaska, backpacking through Europe, following the Grateful Dead for twelve shows in a row. We camped in a junkyard in Indiana. We hiked through rain in Costa Rica and were engaged to be married beneath an active volcano. But somehow this was different, a new kind of risk. I feel like a tree yanked

6 Go through the motions of life. Hold hands. Talk about work. Don't talk about work.
7 Point to marriage on the horizon when you need something to blame. Gesture toward the future. Pose for photos on a cliff somewhere.

loose, my roots swinging around wildly, searching for the right soil.

DESCENT

We drop over the crater rim early one morning, before the gates have opened to the public. Our day off—so it hurts to be here at all. But we've stood on the rim and talked about the crater for months without ever hiking to the bottom. Liability prevents any tourists from taking that trail; and management certainly won't let us do it on the clock. So this morning we use the same rocky trail that Jeff Bridges stumbled down in the movie, *Starman*.[8] The crater now seems a natural meeting place for alien craft. We press our hands against layers of rock we've only pointed out and talked about with tourists. Coconino, Kaibab, and Moenkopi. And it's true the crater floor does feel something like I imagine the surface of the moon must feel—soft and dusty, the bottom of a bowl in the open desert. Our feet sink into the white Coconino dust, leaving our tracks next to rabbit and fox. We stand beneath the massive boiler— just barely the size of a bus, its iron feet moored to concrete pillars sunk deep in the powder. We gaze up at the blue sky ballooning above us, as if we are sitting in a teacup thrust up through the heavens, floating alone in the bright blue atmosphere, happy as meteors. Silence fills the crater as we walk the floor. Old mining timbers and the foundations of shacks, the shiny silver chunk of airplane fuselage with a few faded numbers left. We haven't come to the bottom here—but a new beginning. The decision has been made. Six weeks and we'll be at nine thousand feet, new elevated air. We'll be closer still

---

8 Remember the scene of helicopters chasing him, swarming over the high desert. The alien just wants to go home.

to the stars, living in the sky; and we'll think back to this soft walk across the crater floor, remembering a new lunar bounce to our steps.

High Maintenance

PAGE TURNER

This world is cold and smothered with snow. Everything's in danger of slipping away. On the surface, two nights a week I carry the emergency pager for *Four Seasons Lodging* in Breckenridge, Colorado. It's a cell phone hooked up to the Tannenbaum Condominiums after-hours number. I am the on-call Maintenance Man. My job is to take care of any problems with late check-ins or maintenance emergencies. My job is to make tourists feel at home, safe, secure, and pampered. My job is to save the guests from noise and clogs and minor inconveniences—to make them feel as if the real world is far away.

Most nights the phone never rings. If it does, it's usually a new arrival who can't figure out where his condo is located. Some of the calls I can handle without leaving the house by just telling them where to turn, where to park, and where to find their keys in the check-in box. If I do leave home it's usually just to open a door for a drunk who locked himself out of his room.

So it's not really an "emergency" pager most nights but an "annoyance" pager; my emotional investment in their drama is generated more from a sense of duty than it is from genuine concern. A few times people have water issues—leaks or clogs—that require me to bring tools. These are the exciting calls. The rest of them are mostly forgettable and irritating—a good test of whether I'm married to the job or not.

The truth is that I dislike carrying the pager right from the start. I treat each call with respect, but it's not a role I want to inhabit often. I just don't enjoy being "on call" for tourists. I don't like the parenting feel of it. It makes me feel edgy and nervous. It makes me feel like a servant, a slave to its digital twitter rather than a savior. I stare at it obsessively, waiting for it to ring, hoping it won't.

It's a weeknight, mid-season, and I'm sleeping next to my fiancé with the pager on the counter in the kitchen. Snow is piling up on the steps, burying our cars. It's quiet up where we live, just below tree line. The ringer goes off at 10:30, jerking me from my REM patterns. I stumble into the kitchen in my boxer shorts and pick it up. The keypad glows green and flashes as it rings.

"Helluh," I mumble, "Fur Seasn's Lodging. Thisis Steve."

"Uh, hi," a soft male voice responds. The voice has a Texas drawl. "Yeah, I'm over here at the Trail's End condominiums, number 542, and, well, we got a problem with our bathtub."

I shake the fog out of my head and rub a fist into my eye. "What sort of problem, sir?"

"Well, see," he pauses, "it won't drain."

"It's not draining?"

"No, see. We have some blood in the bathtub and, well, it won't go down."

At first I think I've misheard him. I wait for some kind of explanation. But nothing comes from the voice.

"Excuse me?" I ask.

"Yeah, we have some blood in our bathtub and I just can't get it to drain and I was thinking y'all might be able to help. I didn't know who else to call."

I didn't know what to say. I'm pretty sure there was someone else he could've called.

It's a sick joke, probably John D. messing with me; but there's something about the man's voice, an easy soft quality to it, an honest tone that keeps me on the line. There's something about his call that reconnects me with my self again, a weight that drags me back firmly in the moment. I haven't felt this alive in some time. Someone needs me.

"Are you there?" he asks. "I just need some help."

This is what does it to me. A call of distress. He needs the Maintenance Man. He needs my help, needs salvation. I am necessary now, much more now than just a voice on the phone or a toilet-fixing snow-shoveling maintenance grunt. I matter. At least for now.

Against all common sense or good judgment I respond, "I'll be right there."

I return to the bedroom and kiss my fiancé on the forehead. She stirs slightly and I tell her it's nothing to worry about. I don't explain the call, the blood in the bathtub, those minor details. Because she would tell me not to go. She would warn me, and she would be right to do so. What sort of future husband or father runs off in the middle of the night to help a stranger get blood out of his bathtub? But for some reason I don't want to hear this. I just want to follow the impulse. I just want the certainty of this work.

I get dressed, slip on my boots, grab my pocketknife and climb into my truck. I'm surprisingly calm, unafraid, and more curious than anything as I make my way down the mountain, into town. As much as possible, I follow established tracks through the fresh snow, but they're starting to fill, smooth out, and disappear. The plow won't come until morning. I pick up the phone a couple of times, think about calling someone, but just set it back down on the seat next to me. The stars are so bright tonight they're screaming and the moon shines luminous as a giant street lamp. Some moments, I think, are the kind of moments that bring the blurry bits into focus, that give definition to your present predicament and shape your future in ways that are both inevitable and unpredictable.

DEEP IN THE TREES

My fiancé and I only share one day off a week together and it's often filled with errands to the grocery store or the Wal-Mart in Frisco, maybe the soul-crushing experience of wedding planning. *Plastic chairs or wooden? Chicken or pork? Centerpieces?* Life isn't always easy in this beautiful place. Last night as the snow swirled past the windows, I sipped my beer and watched individual flakes caught and illuminated briefly by the floodlights, but she wanted to fight. So we had a huge fight over the dishes. It was pretty much the same fight we always have, almost like a ritual sparring. We played our roles well. This is how it goes:

F: You never do the dishes. You don't do anything. Ever. And I have to come home and wash all the fucking dishes.

M: Yeah, right. I don't do anything except work manual labor for 40 hours a week.

F: When was the last time you did the dishes? You just put your plate in the sink like I'm some kind of maid.

Jegs, the landlord's German shepherd, started barking. You could hear him beneath the window. Someone must've been walking up the road. Or maybe he heard the rising voices. Maybe he knew.

M: I cook all the meals. All of them. When was the last time you cooked a meal? Maybe we should switch for a week or two.

F: Fine. Great. I can cook.

I try not to say something obnoxious about how Velveeta Shells & Cheese doesn't count as cooking, but sometimes when we're fighting, songs run through my head. I don't know if it's a defense mechanism or an escape or what. In the middle of a fight I'll hear, "You Can't Always Get What You Want," by the Rolling Stones, or "Back Where We Started," by the Kinks, and I'll think *here we go round again*.

We do this on our day off together. Again and again. We do it too much. I think both of us are scared—frightened of the future, scared to be married—and this is how we dance around it.

My other day off I usually choose to go snowboarding alone, without my fiancée or friends. It's not bad, really. Not like you might think. It's quiet in the trees, where I like to ride. Nobody asks me for anything; and I need my alone time. The powder is deepest there, up to my waist on good days; and the crashes don't hurt unless you hit a tree. Most people are still asleep at that hour—the people who depend on me for maintenance.

Back in the deep pockets of powder, I float inches

above the ground on a cushion of air, carving new tracks through the deep stuff. And when you're as big and clumsy as I am, these brief pioneering bursts of weightlessness cannot be underestimated. Some days I get a little lost in the trees, deeper than I should go, because I'm trying to disappear. Life here is beginning to grate on me, grinding me down to a grumpy nub, barely recognizable as a human.

RISING ACTION

Before I make it to Trails End and the blood in the bathtub, I have to stop into Tannenbaum and pick up my plumbing tools. The office is dark, cluttered, and it smells of mop water and cleaning supplies. I look again at the phone, consider calling my boss, Russ, or maybe the police, and then decide against it. I grab the plumbing snake and pipe wrenches, and make a quick exit. I drive to Trails End and park in the underground garage. I ride the elevator up to the fifth floor and stroll down the carpeted hallway to number 542.

I knock on the door, expecting the gentleman with the Texas accent to answer. I wait for a few moments and then knock again. Nothing. No movement, no rustling, not a sound. For some reason this silence scares me.

I can't exactly say why I'm here in the first place—some desperate mix of curiosity and duty, a reaching for something elusive and meaningful—but at the very least I expected someone to greet me, someone who needs my help. I knock again and wait. Nothing.

I pull out my master keys and open the door. I stick

my head inside. "Helloooo," I holler, "Maintenance Man. Anyone home?"

The place is empty. Quiet. Dark. But it's also clean, well-kept, and organized. No signs of a struggle. No blood on the floor, no broken windows. No knives, guns or piles of cocaine.

I push the door open. "Helloooo."

Blood in the bathtub and it won't go down.

That's what the man said. I am a Maintenance Man and I fix things. I maintain Vacationland. I help people enjoy their bubble. I can do this. I make my way down the hall to the first floor bathroom, reach in, flip on the light, expecting … what? … I don't know. Carnage? Blood and guts? The remnants of a chainsaw murder? It could be anything or nothing. But the bathroom is spare and clean, the tub empty and white.

I exit the first floor bath and walk up the stairs to the second-floor loft area, where the master bedroom is located. I reach the bathroom first, but stop just outside the door. I flip on all the lights in the bedroom and take a quick look around. Not a soul in sight. Nobody hiding, waiting to brain me with a golf club or sink a hatchet deep into my sternum. No sign of a bloody struggle. No stains on the mattress. This is a relief.

I back up and turn the corner into the bathroom. I flip on the light and make my way over to the tub. I take one look down into the tub, my eyes settling on the area around the drain and there it is—a mass of blood, chunks of flesh the size of guppies or minnows. The white porcelain dotted with tiny red specks. I take a step back.

Did I just see what I think I saw?

I step back up to the tub and look again. I can't tell what it is, really. Nothing recognizable. No ears or fingers or anything like that. Just blood and slivers of tissue—internal-looking tissue, not skin—tiny filets of fish, like sushi. Yeah, that's what it is. Sushi. Just raw fish marinating in tomato sauce. Food. Easy. I can handle this. I can maybe even fix things and find my way back home. I step away, take a deep breath, and lay out my tools on the vanity. This isn't going to be easy.

SEASONAL HELP

My father taught me everything I know about using tools and fixing things. He taught me how to solve problems. But for me the challenge has never been physical. I can pound a nail, drill a hole, tighten and loosen screws, nuts, and bolts. The challenge for me in maintenance has always been mental, a matter of patience. It's difficult for me to surrender my will to a stripped screw or a closet door that just won't stay on its damn track. I just grind and bash away at it until it's beaten and useless. But this job is teaching me to relax, to listen and breathe and learn from the problem. You have to let the toilet teach you. You have to be—as my dad always said—smarter than the machine. You have to understand how something works before you can understand why it's broken; and you have to let go of your control issues to be a good Maintenance Man.

All of this is hard for me.

I've seen what this place can do to you. I've seen how it sucks you in and down and makes it hard to leave. I've seen the line of cars making tracks over Hoosier

Pass—all the workers who can't afford to live in the town where they make a living. I read a story in the paper about the man and his dog and how they found a dead baby in a plastic bag, buried beneath a pile of rocks, just steps away from condos and the hiking path.

He said it "looked like eggplant," until he noticed an ear, and I thought about the loneliness and isolation a woman must feel to do something like that. "Probably stillborn," the County Coroner said. "Probably a seasonal worker," everyone said as if that explained something.

They call them "seasonal" here, as if they are part of the weather, a temporary and transient phenomena that blows through the valley. They mean someone with no support system, no family, no money, no choice. They mean they have no home here. They just work here. We all just work here. You just visit. Nobody really lives here.

BACK TO THE BLOOD

At this moment I sort of drift outside of myself and watch as my sense of duty takes over, my Maintenance Man identity overriding all others, and, for some reason, I decide to see if I can get the blood and tissue to wash down the drain. This seems right to me. Just make the problem disappear. That's the answer. I am the Maintenance Man. I am a problem solver.

The water splatters into the tub and the stuff washes back up the tub, mixing with the water and then slides back down the porcelain, hanging up in the drain-trap. Clouds of red ooze out from the tissue, mixing with the water. This isn't working, but I'm smart enough not to touch it.

I should be thinking about preserving samples or evidence or something. I should leave. I should call the police. I should get back home, back to my own identity, back to the minor inconveniences of every day life, back to the roles we all play everyday. I have to accept that I can't fix everything. I barely understand what I'm seeing. But that doesn't stop me from trying.

I run the water again and check the drain-trap. No hair. No significant clogs. I'm just doing my job. And then some of the reality of this moment hits me again. I'm standing over a bathtub with bloody chunks of flesh and it's quite possible that I'm helping whoever is responsible get rid of the evidence, leaving my fingerprints all over the place.

"Fuck this," I finally say to myself and throw an old rag-towel over the mess, not thinking that I was, at that moment, leaving evidence that I'd been there, that I was somehow involved with this. I take a step back, gather up my plumbing tools, and turn around.

"Ahhhhh!" I scream.

A pale thin-haired man in a yellow cardigan sweater stands in the doorway.

"Hi," he says with a Texas drawl.

"Holy shit," I say, bending over to catch the breath he knocked out of me. "You scared the crap out of me."

I have no idea where he came from. I didn't hear a door open or anything. No footsteps. He just appeared out of the darkness.

"Oh, I'm sorry," he says and sort of steps out of

the doorway, back into the shadows.

At this point I'm convinced this guy in his yellow cardigan sweater has come to finish me off, maybe add to the collection of corpses he's keeping in the kitchen. I can see his hands. He doesn't seem to be wielding an axe or a butcher knife or a chainsaw, but he does look eerily like a cross between Mr. Rogers and Hannibal Lecter. Maybe he wants to eat my face and sing a song about it.

He smiles and a quick shiver runs up my spine. I don't want to talk. I just want to get out of here and get back home.

"Uh, there's really nothing I can do about that," I say, moving around him, out the door, never turning my back. "We'll have to call a plumber in the morning. Or someone to …um … take care of it."

At this point I'm moving like I'm electrified and I don't ask for an explanation and he doesn't offer one.

He just stands there smiling. "OK, sure," he says softly, his hands gathered up below his waist, fingers laced together. "I'm sorry about that mess."

"Oh, that's OK," I say, breathing hard now. I turn and start down the stairs. "Just leave it for now," I call over my shoulder.

I'm at the bottom of the stairs now but I don't stop. I don't wait for him to come after me. "You have a nice night, sir," I say as I push the door open and step into the hallway. My toolbox bangs on the door-jamb. I don't wait for his response before I'm down the hall, practically running. I skip the elevator and take the stairs, bounding three steps at a time, and soon I'm in the parking garage, scrambling to find my keys. I unlock my door, climb into my truck, throw it into reverse, and don't really breathe until I'm out of the parking lot, on the road back home, back to my fiancé and my real life.

When I crawl back into bed, she stirs awake. "Everything OK?"

"Plumbing problem," I say. "I'll tell you all about it in the morning."

I do not call the police. I do not call anyone. I do not have a good explanation for this decision. I do not think about what might have happened in that condo or what might have happened to me. I simply crawl into bed and go to sleep.

CHICKEN EXIT

I figured that marriage and graduate school would be my excuse to leave the Blue Valley of Colorado, that it'd be my chicken exit from this rollercoaster way of life. It's exciting here for sure; but some days you get tired of gripping tight with your teeth as you plow through a dip into a loop. We were supposed to leave. This was the plan. One year here and then we quietly take our exit and move on to serious business, the stuff of adulthood. Marriage, graduate school, a dog, then children. That's how it goes. But I somehow manage to miss most of the deadlines for graduate school. I send off late applications, call and beg forgiveness; but it's not looking good for me. I blow it—perhaps intentionally. My chances are slim.

I'm close to giving up, close to committing myself to the life, the identity of the Maintenance Man. I call the schools where I had deferred my admission a year earlier, expecting them to beg me to come, and they barely recognize my name. It becomes increasingly clear that I've missed that train. I have no real plans now, nothing for certain. No escape routes mapped out this time. We decide to stay another season in the mountains.

When a school calls and offers me late admission to their program, I accept but I defer my admission for a year. Again.

My fiancé and I seem to be in a constant state of deferral, living one day to the next, our future looming on the horizon—following a pattern we'll learn to repeat, a skill I hope we can develop through stumble, stab, flame, and miss. I understand that I have to learn to live with what I can't understand, can't fix, can't maintain, and sometimes just step back and watch it move and shake and crash without me. Sometimes the world is bigger than you and your personal shit. Sometimes there's nothing you can do but go along for the ride.

DENOUEMENT

When I show up for work the morning after the blood in the bathtub, I don't have a story to tell. I don't have an explanation and I don't plan to offer one. Everyone is there at the office—Ben, John D, and Stinky—just getting ready to go out for a morning of shoveling. I'm prepared to keep my silence until my supervisor, Stinky asks me, "Any action on the pager last night?"

Here we go, I think.

Stinky's real name is Steve; but his breath is so gut-wrenchingly bad that everyone just calls him "Stinky."

"No, not really," I say, "Why?"

He tells me how there were ambulances and police cars at Trails End last night. "All over the place," he says. "Crazy stuff."

"So what happened?" I ask, playing dumb, hoping for an answer.

"Well," Stinky says, takes a big sip of his coffee, and sort of settles back into his chair. He acts like he knows. He tells me how a tourist staying in Trails End 542 had somehow torn a hole in his esophagus and had been swallowing blood and tissue. The guy had vomited it up in the bathtub at the condo and then passed out before his friends called 911. The ambulance took the guy down to a hospital in Denver. He was in pretty bad shape.

"Nearly died," Stinky says.

I hesitate. This is it.

I could just keep my mouth shut.

But I don't.

"Yeah, I know," I say.

"I was there."

"What?" Stinky rocks forward in his chair and sets his coffee mug on the desk.

"I mean, I didn't know what happened, but the guy's friend called me late last night and told me he had blood in his bathtub and couldn't get it to wash down," I pause at the sight of chins dropping, all eyes focusing on me.

"And, well, I went down there last night. I saw it. But the guy didn't tell me anything."

"What did you see?" Ben asks, his lip already curling at the thought.

"Blood for sure," I say "But also some chunks of flesh or tissue or something. It looked like fish."

78

"It looked like sushi," I clarify.

"And you didn't call the police?" John D asks.

"Nope," I say.

"You went down there?" Stinky asks, his eyes wide with disbelief.

"What were you thinking?" John D asks and I realize, for the first time in a long time, that I can't answer this question. I wasn't thinking. I was just acting.

"I don't really know," I say.

And that's the end of it.

This is true. Still today I can't say for sure what drew me to that voice, that call for help, what made me think I could fix things; and I wonder if it was just a morbid sense of curiosity, like a private car wreck I'd been invited to witness or if I honestly thought I could help. I could have shirked my Maintenance Man duties and ignored the call. I could have called the police but I chose not to. I chose to face this situation alone. I didn't know for sure what these choices said about me. I only knew that I had made them consciously, deliberately, and that sort of clarity had been missing in my life for a while.

When that call came I felt like I'd been sucked into a story, something bigger than me—a strange and bizarre tale of blood and intrigue and yellow cardigan sweaters—and I couldn't figure out what it meant. I tried to fix things, but I failed. It was beyond my capabilities; and I couldn't get smarter than the machine.

My life felt that way too some days—like it was bigger than me, an ancient story moving with a momentum impossible to match. I can't tell you exactly why I decided to go to that room that night, or why

I didn't tell anyone about what I saw until the next day. I also can't really tell you why I just drove home and crawled into bed or why I would get married later that summer. And I wish that I could tell you that in that moment, I knew somehow that it would all end, inevitably. I wish I knew, as I draped an arm over my fiancé, that despite years of honest effort, our marriage would not last.

But I didn't. Not yet. I only knew that a call for help had come and I had responded. I'd tried to fix things, to make everyone happy, but I didn't have the right tools. Perhaps if that night had given me a window into our future I would have laid awake tossing and turning. Perhaps I would have paced the floors, my feet dragging heavy with the weight of realization. But instead I propped the Emergency phone up on the nightstand, kissed my fiancé goodnight, and closed my eyes. Outside the window a new snow was falling, a thick blanket spreading out and muffling the noise of the world, smoothing over my tracks back to work.

I'm Just Getting To
The Disturbing Part

At this point in my story, this much I know for sure: It's summer, 1998, Fort Collins, Colorado, and I'm way too old . . . or way too big for a pink plastic Barbie pool. I'm twenty-seven, ten years removed from the best-shape-of-my-life, and at 6'4", 250 lbs, even if I sit cross-legged and squeeze my knees together with my elbows, I can only manage to get my ankles and rear-end wet.

When I sit down most of the water rises up and spills out, soaking into the brittle grass. I flop around in the pool and realize—vaguely at first, in the way that you realize your fly is open only by the way people are staring at your crotch—that to a passerby I probably look like a hairless wildebeest rolling around in a puddle on the hot savannah, a tanker-ship in dry-dock, a square peg in a round hole. I look like a jerk just wasting water. But I don't care how I appear, because even a little water can save you in this heat.

My wife points at me and laughs—one of those big toothy wide-mouth laughs. "Oh my God," she says, "You're hilarious."

It seems cruel. But she has room to laugh. She's tiny, about half my size. She fits in the pool just fine. It's positively luxurious for her. She floats like a water bug on her back, paddling her little legs around and mocking me. "That's just wrong," I say when she shows off by submerging her entire body. She splashes me playfully as she climbs out and the water feels so cold on my skin that it burns, leaving a smattering of wet fire across my legs and belly.

After a few failed attempts at cooling off, I finally figure out that the only way for me to soak my whole body is to fill the Barbie pool to the brim, squat down beside it, and then fall into the water, letting it splash over me and out onto the grass. My best friend has to do the same thing, but he's 3 inches taller than me and skinny and he looks like a giant gawky heron flailing in a backyard birdbath.

We're out here because it's hot. And we need to be saved. This is what's important in the story.

Did I mention this: It's the middle of July, and all along the Front Range of Colorado we're suffering the sort of summer heat that burns when you inhale, singeing nose-hair and scalding your sinus cavities; the particular brand of intense abusive heat where your brain seems to expand inside your skull and you feel a little dumber, slower, and sleepier; the kind of heat that makes you see things funny—watery mirages, floating apparitions, ghosts of the everyday.

We have chosen this day, this Hell-hot broiling weekend, to make our final move down to the Front Range of Colorado from Breckenridge—high up in the Blue Valley at 9,000 feet, where the air is thin and cool, the kind of air they name deodorants after—Mountain Fresh, Cool Breeze, etc.

We loaded up the last loads of household junk and hauled it the 160 miles between apartments. We unpacked last night and sweated our way to sleep on the soft furnished mattress in our new apartment. We have no air-conditioning. I tossed and turned all night, positioning and re-positioning box fans to get the maximum whirlwind effect—all of it ultimately futile—and I finally rose at dawn, dug our coffee maker out of a box, and made a pot of dark French roast. I drank the whole thing and brewed another.

My wife and I rented this 1 bedroom place in Fort Collins just a half-block from the University where I will be attending graduate school for writing, a place that is also a short drive from another University where my wife will begin her masters and certification in education. Conveniently, my best friend since junior-high school and his girlfriend rented the apartment right next door.

He's recovering from a botched hernia operation and volunteering with the Larimer County wild-land fire crew, taking courses at the community college. His girlfriend is clerking for a judge in the County Court. We're all sort of in-between things or just starting something new, definitely in a period of proverbial flux; and we're still getting used to the changes.

Heat is just one of the new challenges. Our apartments are poorly ventilated and stifling. So this morning my friend and I drove out to *Toys R' Us* and bought a pink plastic Barbie pool, the only model they had left. We brought it home, filled it up using a garden hose, and now we're all sitting around it in the backyard in green vinyl lawn chairs, half-naked, our feet dipped in the water, taking turns soaking and refilling the pool.

We try not to think about the fact that it's 75 degrees in Breckenridge—sunny but with a cool breeze and that mountain-crisp air—where we all recently lived and where we all, on some level, still wish we were living. We don't do the math. We don't think about the difference in comfort level that 30 degrees makes. The radio said it could get up to 110 today on the Front Range; and that's just not right. There's a drought and Horsetooth Reservoir is drying up. There've been news reports about the retreat of water. The other day, it had resided so far they found a dead dog in the mud with cinder blocks tied to its feet. We told ourselves that someone must have tried to put a sick dog out of its misery. There wasn't much left of it—mostly bones and skin, hair and teeth.

It isn't fair, this oppressive heat. It does bad things to your head. Hot weather makes me grumpy.

I feel swollen and bloated, oozing with sweat, like a fat sausage roasting on a grill. We try to distract ourselves with booze and food and small-talk; but eventually we hit one of those awkward pauses in the conversation, a heat-induced lull that leaves each of us foul-faced and pissy, all thinking the same thing—we gotta get out of this heat before someone gets hurt.

Suddenly my friend's face brightens. "You guys want to take my kayak out to Horsetooth?"

A collective sigh releases from the group and smiles spread around the pink pool.

"Oh yeah, maybe do some swimming?" my wife pipes in.

Three heads nod in unison.

But the attorney says, "I'm pretty sure swimming is illegal there."

"No way," I protest. "Why?"

"It's dangerous, I guess," she says.

"But its soooo hot," my wife says.

"Let's just go," my friend says. "It's gotta be better than this." He gestures at the half-empty Barbie bath, bits of grass and dirt floating around, our feet lurking below the surface like pale fish; and in no time we are loading his fiberglass banana-colored kayak onto the roof of his jeep and emptying the pool-water in the yard.

Let me tell you what I don't know at this point in my story: I will be afraid of water. It will happen a few years from here. This will be a new fear that develops unexpectedly, and it will be hard for me even to admit, difficult to reconcile with my childhood love of water. But one day I'll be walking along the Poudre River in Fort Collins with my three-year-old son (a boy who will be born and brought home to a house just two blocks away from this very apartment with the pink Barbie pool) and the water in the river will be moving fast, running as high as I've ever seen it after two full days of rain rolling down from the mountains.

The boy will be the kind of child who likes to get down close and throw rocks in the water, his toes often dipped in at the edge, soaking his kiddie-Vans up to the Velcro straps. I will look at him down by the rushing river, and then up at the swirling brown force moving past and I'll be seized with irrational gut-dropping panic.

I know this now.

Like a brush fire, my imagination will flare up, burst, leap, and I'll picture him falling into the river, bobbing up a couple of times, and disappearing beneath the churn. I'll hear my own footsteps on the bank, running helplessly and then watch myself dive into the water after him, swim down, deep, searching. I'll go with him. And before I know it the fire of my thoughts will smolder, tamp, and I'll be back to the present future, nervously chewing my fingernails down to nothing and gripping his hand tight, pulling him back from the water, up to the path, away from my fears. He'll try to wiggle free from my grasp as he reaches for a rock. He'll always be wiggling away.

"I want to throw a rock in that wave, Daddy," he'll say plaintively, pointing at a cascade of foamy brown water pouring over a partially submerged tree.

"I know, buddy. But you have to hold my hand. It's like crossing the street. You always have to hold Daddy's hand when you're near the river."

"Why, Daddy?"

"Because it's dangerous. See how fast the river is moving. If you fell in you could die."

This is true, but I should find a better way to say it. I don't want to plant fears in the loamy soil of his consciousness. I don't want him to think about dying.

"Because you could drown," I'll say and pause, trying to shift the conversation away from this topic, "because it's dangerous. Just trust me, OK?"

"OK, Daddy," he'll say, and I know that he means it.

We'll walk a little further along the river and I'll try to tell him about "eddy" currents and how they move backwards, against the flow of the main current, bits of flotsam and detritus swirling in the spin of story. We'll stop to watch several lines and tails spinning madly off of the main push, catching up twigs and debris, spawning tiny whirlpools; but he mostly just wants to throw rocks at the surface of this scene, this image, this day. I'll still want him to be amazed and curious about water. I'll still want him to find things about rivers that aren't scary. But the fear will still be there, lurking beneath the surface of these casual interactions.

"Eddy," the boy will say, "That's silly."

"That's your grandpa's name," I'll say.

"I know that, Daddy," he'll say impatiently because he already knows how things come back again.

The boy will be naturally curious about the most dangerous things—waterfalls and ripples, noisy whitewater and submerged limbs, all the stuff beneath the surface of these days. I want to let him explore. I want to let go, let him learn to swim and survive and all that—but I will have developed this fear of water like I've never had before. It's just there, taking up space, weighing me down; and I don't want to give this burden to my son.

I think I always believed that as I grew older and matured, I'd shed phobias like old luggage or clothes—and I have lost a few along the way. But I never imagined that I'd get mossy-green with new fears as the years progressed.

This one. This new fear of water. I can trace it back.

It starts at Horsetooth Reservoir on a miserable hot day in July.

Here is what should be clear by now. We are not alone in the water. Dozens of like-minded people have come to Horsetooth to escape the heat. But the lake is a place of sacrifice. What you gain in water, you lose in shade. What you gain in depth, you lose in vision.

There are few trees here, so people have set up large shade canopies and bright blue Igloo coolers surround the perimeters like colorful sandbags. The dusty parking lot is crammed with cars. Boats and Jet-Skis buzz up and down the lake, in and out of Satanka Cove, where the public dock is located and many people have camped or squatted for the day along the banks, taking occasional illegal dips into the water. Some openly flout the posted warnings against swimming in the cove. We try to be subtle by sitting close to the edge and slipping in just to cool off. We take turns going out in the boat, paddling out into the larger lake and splashing each other.

It's still hot but it beats the Barbie pool.

The landscape around Satanka Cove is harsh and terracotta red with slabs of uprooted sandstone rising all around like the plates of a buried stegosaurus. In the water, we paddle past striated shelves of crumbling shale. There is no beach, no sand. Just mud and rocks. But there is water and it is cool. We take a few turns and my friend and I sit on the bank watching the women paddle back up to the edge. We are waiting for our second turn out. They beach the boat and we strap on life jackets. My friend climbs in and I'm helping my wife out, on to the bank, taking her life jacket, when we hear a voice calling to us, an anguished voice.

"Heeeelllp," she calls.

We turn and see a woman in a tank top and jean-shorts running toward us. She is screaming and waving her arms around. "Heelllp," she calls out again. I look behind her, expecting to see something or someone chasing her, but there's nothing.

She runs up to us. My friend sits in the boat. The woman is panting, trying to catch her breath. "He went under," she barks, "He went under and he's not coming up." She turns and points to a small inlet off the main water where I'd seen some boys diving from the rocks earlier. "He's not coming up," she repeats then doubles over and puts her hands on her knees.

My friend and I both seem to realize immediately what she is saying.

A boy is drowning. He needs our help.

We look at each other for a second and then take off in the direction from which she came—he in the boat, me running on the bank. He paddles like crazy, stirring up great roils of water. I run hard, my sandals slapping on the rock; and we both reach the inlet about the same time. We are the first ones there besides two other guys standing waist-deep, breathing deeply, staring hopelessly at the water. They are dark-haired and deeply tanned, younger than us by a few years, and appear to be the drowning boy's swimming companions. Beer cans drift past in the water and I get a sense of what they've been doing out here at the lake.

"My brother, man!" one of them says. "He went under."

"What happened?" my friend asks.

"We were swimming across and he started splashing and we thought he was joking," the boy says, staring at the water. "We thought he was joking," he says again.

"Where?" he asks, paddling his boat up close. I am standing on the opposite bank.

"Right fucking there, man!" the other boy says, pointing at a spot in the water.

My friend slips out of his life jacket and rolls out of his boat, into the water. I climb down the bank and slip in over the edge. We both swim out to the area where the boy pointed. We look at each other, take a deep breath, and then dive. Again and again we dive down into the deep-green water, surfacing only long enough to catch our breath.

I try to open my eyes underwater but can't see a thing. I dive down as far as I can go, feeling pockets of cold water as I get closer to the bottom. I hit the mud and sweep my arms and legs out wildly trying to feel his body, hoping to touch his slippery cold flesh or maybe grab an arm. But my lungs will only let me stay down for a second or two before I have to swim hard for the surface. It's deep, maybe 15 or 20 feet or more in spots.

As I break the surface and breech, gasping for air, my friend is quick behind me. We take a moment at the surface and then dive down again. I know how this works. I know that every second, every minute counts and the quicker we can find him, the better chance he has to survive. We dive down repeatedly, finding and feeling nothing. Not a sign. Not a limb. Not a clump of hair or the brush of a swimsuit. Nothing but deep cold water and slippery mud on the bottom. But we keep diving, dipping down below. Over and over again. There is nothing else to do but try.

I break the surface once and see my wife swimming out to me. "Go back," I yell. "Please go back!" I can't bear the thought of losing her. By now there are other people in the water, seven or eight of us now, diving down and searching for him. Boats buzz past. I can hear a helicopter coming, rising up over the foothills. The sky looks wiped, skimmed, ironed like a blue shirt. Steep shale walls shade the cove, so it's cool in here. I dog-paddle, kicking my arms and legs out, knifing through the green, and try to breathe deeply, evenly.

A woman in a blue bikini stands on a fishing boat screaming, "Does everyone have a buddy? You need to have a buddy!!"

I look at my old friend.

She means a swim buddy.

We swim to the bank and pull ourselves up on the rocks. We've been diving for almost twenty minutes. We sit there, breathing hard, exhausted and weak. We look out at the crew of divers and a boat drifting slowly. Blue Bikini's husband has a sonar fish-finder. Someone said we should use it; so now he's trolling back and forth across the inlet.

It's too late, I think.

The helicopter's blades go *thwop-thwop-thwop*, punctuating the air, echoing off the walls of the cove, and it lands lightly just above the boat ramp, kicking up a cloud of white dust.

Suddenly the guy in the boat stops. "Right there," he says, pointing down at his fish-finder and then at the water. "There's something big and it's not moving."

The gaggle of divers kicks and paddles furiously over to the spot and, one by one, each of them disappears under the water like a cormorant. My friend and I slip back in and swim out to the spot. We take deep breaths and dive under again, only to pop back up moments later without ever reaching the bottom. My dog paddle looks more like tired flailing than anything resembling a swim stroke.

"It's deep," I sputter. "I can't touch."

"Me neither."

Just then a thin wiry boy of maybe 17 or 18 breeches and hollers, "I touched him. I felt him lying down there, but I can't pull him up. It's too deep."

Another swimmer says, "Let's try again," and the two of them disappear.

We make another effort, but I can't get down that deep. I am exhausted, my lungs aching and my limbs all rubbery. We swim back to the bank. I look up and see my wife sitting on the opposite bank. She has her arms crossed over her knees and her head down.

"How long?" I ask, shivering from the cold water.

"I don't know," my friend says, "Must be close to a half-hour."

"Too long," I say.

"He's gone," he says.

We hear the emergency vehicles approaching, their sirens rising and falling with the surrounding terrain until they come screaming down into Satanka Cove. They slip their Rescue boat in the water and are upon us in seconds, plowing into the cove and pushing a wide white wake ahead of them. They order everyone out of the water and a diver in a full wetsuit drops over the edge of the boat. We all wait on the bank for what seems like hours; but it's only a minute or so before the water bubbles, roils, and the diver pushes the boy up through the surface, breaking the thin skin of water that separates us from the deep.

His body thumps loudly against the fiberglass boat. He is fish-limp and heavy with full lungs. They work furiously on him from the minute he's in the boat, trying to revive him, but by the time they get back to the ramp and we have made our way over to the scene, the boy has been loaded into the helicopter and spirited away. He is dead. Everyone seems to know this, and there isn't much to be said about it.

The boy's brother is there, the one who was standing in the water when we first arrived. He looks dazed, confused. A wet towel drapes over his shoulders. Nobody asks us anything. No questions. No clarifications. I'm not sure what I expect, but I keep thinking that we'll need to give a statement or something.

I approach the brother, "I'm so sorry," I say. "I don't know what to say," and then I reach out and try to give him a hug but it goes all wrong and we sort of half-embrace, each of us getting one arm up and around the other, then quickly separating. He doesn't speak a word. He doesn't seem to recognize me at all. I just stand there, watching him take the long walk up the grey concrete boat-ramp; and I feel a cold chill rattle up and down my spine, knowing it's no comfort in the heat of this day.

Here is what I haven't told you up to this point in my story: My brother died when he was eighteen—killed in his car, slammed into a tree, head smashed in—a violent noisy sort of death. Totally unlike a drowning. He was just a kid too.

This is how it all comes around again—moments and words caught up in the eddy current of back-story and memory.

They say that you experience euphoria as you are drowning, at least for a moment; but I've always wondered when this comes. At what point? Is it the euphoria of surrender or something else that water does to the brain? And how exactly would they know? I suppose they interview people who have been pulled back to the surface and revived, given a chance to tell their story.

My brother never had a chance at euphoria. He couldn't have told any stories if he survived. His brain was too bruised, too battered and crushed. I imagine that he believed right up to the end that he could survive, that he would make it, and it hurts me to think he fought it. It hurts to know that I'm the only one who can tell his story.

When we're near the water—any water now—I'm completely paranoid and overprotective of my children. I'm afraid of the possibility, the subtle menace below the surface of a stream, crick, river, pond, or kiddie pool. My son is competent in the water, but not a natural swimmer or athlete. It helps me to think people can survive being underwater. They can be pulled back. There is a window there, between life and death, and it can last as long as 45 minutes in cold temperatures. I remind myself of this—those stories of kids being pulled from beneath the ice of a frozen lake and revived—and sometimes it works as a kind of psychological salve. Sometimes it helps tamp down the flare of these new father fears.

When my son was younger, before he knew how to swim, we'd go swimming together and he'd cling to my neck like a baby monkey and not let go. When I tried to get him to dog paddle on his own, his eyes locked onto me, his face stricken with fear. I held him out at arms-length; and he lifted his little chin desperately above the surface, squawking, "DADDY DADDY DADDY!" and it nearly broke my heart every time. I knew that we just needed to spend more time in the water for him to get used to it and feel comfortable—but sometimes I wondered if I really wanted them to get completely comfortable around water.

I worry now that I will pass my new fear on to my children, that they will inherit it like a great and heavy piece of furniture that they must lug from house to house for the rest of their lives. I don't want them to carry the weight of my fears or they'll never learn to swim on their own, never shed the heft of my pathologies, and never experience the simple fun of gliding through the aqua blue weightless world of a swimming pool, skimming their bodies along the bottom and breaking the surface like a silver fish.

Here's the disturbing part: When that rescue diver pushed that drowned boy up through the skin of water, I couldn't be sure it wasn't my brother's body thumping on the fiberglass hull of the boat. I know it sounds strange, but I experienced some kind of transference in the water that day at Horsetooth Reservoir. As the time dragged on and I knew the boy's life was slipping away, I felt as if I was slipping closer to my brother. I couldn't stop thinking about him. Every dive down was a dive closer to him. I felt his presence down there, in the dark and quiet green water, as if *he* was that boy on the bottom, waiting for me to pull him back up again.

Perhaps I felt something close to the other side, the chill of death in that deep green water; and I understood how quickly you can cross over—especially below the surface. I was afraid to open my eyes, afraid of what I might see—a smile, a wave, a tassel of hair, the bright neon of a swimsuit, or my brother's face. I was afraid part of me might want to stay down there, swimming in the euphoria of surrender, that I might just unhinge my jaw, swallow, and embrace it; and that's where this must have started, a big part of the reason I now lug around this new father-fear of water. It's hard to drop that day into the past, to just let it go in the wash of memory and watch it bob and roll and slip beneath the surface.

Wake-up Calls

1. 2000

Where's the baby? I called out in the dark.

Half asleep, I sat up in bed.

Where's the baby? I asked again.

I'd been troubled recently by dreams of abandonment and forgetting—vague, formless visions and fragments—the only tangible evidence most nights, a sweat-soaked pillow. No clear images or stories I could relate the next morning. But tonight I was awakened by worry over a baby, a child we hadn't really even considered seriously. I called out and my wife mumbled her response;

We don't have a baby.

Then she rolled over and went back to sleep. The dog paced the hall and stood in the door, looking up at me. I could just make out her shape in the shadows. Emptiness settled over the house again and I tried to quiet my trembling brain.

Some nights I wondered if I was still recovering. It had only been a few months since sickness racked my body, leaving me dehydrated from vomiting and suffering non-stop searing headaches that made it nearly impossible to move or sleep or think clearly. It felt as if someone was trying to shove my eyeballs out from the inside. I spent almost a week in the fetal position before I was admitted to hospital, given a spinal tap, and diagnosed with viral meningitis. I couldn't think straight for a while afterward, my brain slowly emerging from the fog of infection. I tired easily, had trouble eating, and lost 17 pounds in two weeks before I started to recover.

Two nights after my baby dream, I sat up in bed again, awakened by a new noise this time. Something loud and sharp. Unusual and shattering. Out of context. Outside and unwanted. I slipped on a robe and walked to the back of the house. I opened the sliding glass door and peered up into a shark-bittten sky, ragged with clouds. The air felt cold on my chest. I heard something out in the street, some kind of commotion. The dog bounced behind me, her hackles stiff, and the neighbor pets howled a warning call.

What could it be?

Who is out there, in the dark?

The eyes of streetlights burned overhead like Orson's alien ships and the air looked like it had been scrubbed clean, shined, and buffed clear, as if I was staring through glass, at the night scene captured in a jar. I walked through the weedy yard, the dog tracking at my heel, and peered around the garage. In the street, a Jeep lay on its side, the wheels exposed to my view. Three boys in baseball caps stood around. Nobody seemed hurt. But I heard one of them say, "It's leaking gas," as another boy dug out his cell-phone.

They'd taken the corner too fast and rolled their Jeep.

We lived at an intersection, a corner where a short side street that fed into a series of boxy apartment complexes T'd into another street. Police sometimes parked on the side street to catch cars speeding down the other one. The corner wasn't an especially noisy corner and it was located across from a large flood-control basin perfect for walking the dog. That night there was nobody else around. Just us and stars.

It was late, well past 2 a.m. and I should have gone back to bed. But I tiptoed closer, barefoot in the wet grass, because I wanted to see more. The boys were lucky the Jeep didn't roll all the way over. I watched them and I could see the panic in their movements, the worry in the way they put their hands to their heads. They were probably drunk and hoping the police didn't show up.

I saw those boys, vulnerable beneath the streetlights, and thought of my own youth gone, the memories of similar misadventures with friends, and I wanted to help. I wanted to tell them to run or rush to their side and help lift the Jeep—which they tried to do without my help, to no avail. I wanted to reach out to them, but I was nearly naked beneath my robe; and I knew that perhaps the best way I could help them was by *not* calling the police.

I watched the boys' friends arrive in a SUV, and the five of them, working quickly, tied a tow-rope to the roll-bar of the Jeep and then used the other truck to pull it back upright. It was an impressive display of teamwork and togetherness, of problem solving and common sense—the sort of things I imagined any father would want for his son; and I felt a strange surge of pride. I wanted to cheer as the boys untied the rope, jumped in the Jeep, started it up, and drove away. The dog and I walked back into the rented house where we lived, not a home so much as a stopping point, an intersection between youth and something else. I moved on my skinned feet, back to my wife, over the night floors dusted with the expectant promise of those words:

We don't have a baby.

I still couldn't shake the language of my wake-up dream, not this night, not with the moon so fat, not with empty rooms calling. Through the sprinkle of broken window glass on the asphalt, I'd seen the tar of my future, thick with hope for a child, and I could not run from it.

2. 2001

In the Summer of 2001, just months before 9/11 would change the world forever, a serial rapist stalked Fort Collins, Colorado, prowling neighborhoods at night, slipping in through open windows, unlocked sliding doors and assaulting women. Everywhere were the sounds of denial:

"Things like this don't happen here."

"I never lock my doors at night."

"It's just too hot. I have to keep the screen door open."

"This is Fort Collins."

Things like this don't happen here.

We lived two blocks from campus in a tiny house with purple trim. I worked an 8-5 job, advising students on how to get into classes or how to appeal a parking ticket or how to avoid getting suspended; and I spent much of my time anticipating, dreading, attending, and loathing the odd theater of office staff meetings.

If I was extremely lucky, I could combine my

caffeine jitters with the occasional sugar rush from a donut or nut-crusted muffin. The more meetings I attended the less and less I said. I made $27,000 a year and thought there was a pretty good chance that I'd be doing that job—or one like it—for the rest of my life. We didn't own a house. We each drove 12 year-old cars and we were up to our necks in credit card debt.

And we were trying to make a baby.

I am a notoriously light sleeper—known to bolt upright in bed at the slightest noise. Always have been. And I'd been thinking a lot about this baby. I felt unsettled. A bit off. Spinning in something of a mental dither.

One night as my wife slept next to me with the windows open—possibly already pregnant--I awoke to the subtle sound of our side gate, rattling and opening, a sound I knew because I'd made it myself thousands of times, a sound I knew intuitively as a harmless, simple sound, but also a sound that my brain, even in a semi-conscious state knew was only harmless in certain contexts.

I looked out the window to see a tall dark figure walk past the frame. I followed him with my eyes as I stood and moved toward the open back door, just a screen door between me and the dark. I wore nothing but a pair of boxer shorts. As he came into view again out the back door, I yelled at the top of my lungs, "Get the fuck out of here. Now, motherfucker!" and the man stumbled, clearly startled by my outburst.

He said, "Whoa, man," then paused, struggling to stand completely upright and said, "Whoa," again.

"Get the fuck out of my yard now, motherfucker!" I barked again.

"What's going on?" my girlfriend asked.

"There's someone in the yard."

"OK, OK, man. Jeez," the man said and lurched toward the back of our yard.

The man was clearly drunk and bewildered. "Goddamnit," I muttered, as I watched him stumble blindly toward the wire fence at the back of the yard. I tried not to laugh when he hit the fence full stride and fell back into the grass like he'd been punched.

It was funny for a moment. But then he got up and walked back toward the house and before I could even start screaming at him again, making as much scary noise as I could muster, he raised his hands in defeat and shuffled back down the side of the house, crashed through the gate, and left it swinging open as he disappeared into the night. I thought about following after him, taking him aside, helping find his house. I didn't want him to get hurt, but I had the news reports rattling around in my head. What if he had been the rapist, and he was searching for an open door? What if I hadn't been home to protect my wife? I called the police and told them that I had just chased a man out of my yard but that I didn't think he was the rapist.

"I think he's just a drunk college student," I told them. "He's probably harmless," I said. Probably someone else's kid. Just trying to find his way home.

"Probably," the voice said.

3. 2002

The night we brought our first-born child home from the hospital, I knew the colors of my world had changed forever. We lived in the same tiny two-bedroom house just a block from campus, located right in the middle of the rowdiest student neighborhood. Just two days old, our son slept for only a couple of hours at a stretch, and it was my turn to be up with him. I checked the clock and turned on the TV. It was 3:00 a.m.. I paced around the small house carrying him in the crook of my arm, bouncing and singing songs, just trying to soothe him back to sleep.

He chortled and I looked down at his red and purple-tinted body, all shriveled up like a tiny old man with these enormous white-socked feet. His neck drooped like a wet noodle; his fists curled into tiny wrinkled balls. The blood in his veins coursed just beneath thin new skin, and the soft spots on his skull pulsed rhythmically with his heartbeat.

The theme song for *Northern Exposure*, one of my favorite shows, had just started when I heard a racket at the side-door—the sound I knew instinctively as someone turning the knob, pushing against the dead-bolt lock, trying to get inside our house.

I looked down at our son and felt this instant click of resolve in my gut, this whir and hum of images, impressions, colors and sounds. I felt suddenly—quite surprisingly—incredibly protective, almost *animal*. My hackles raised, I peeked around the corner, not sure what to expect, my senses tingling, ready for anything.

Standing at the side-door was not a burglar, intruder or rapist, but a pudgy girl in a black hooded sweatshirt—maybe seventeen or eighteen, and quite obviously drunk. I saw her through the glass. She teetered on the porch, methodically turning the knob. I watched her for a few moments, glad the door was locked up tight. She kept turning the knob and pushing her shoulder against the door.

I stepped up and rapped on the glass. The girl

didn't move, didn't even look up at me. I knocked again and she finally locked her wandering gaze onto me. I pointed at the baby curled up in my arm, his tiny red fists clutched up to his chin.

"Wrong house," I said through the glass.

She just stared, squinted her eyes, and then looked down at the baby.

"Wrong house!" I barked.

She threw her hands up in a show of surrender, turned slowly, and fell flat on her face in our flowerbed.

I called the police, laid the baby down in bed next to my wife, and watched the girl through the door until the cops arrived. She lay there in the dirt for a while, then rolled out into the driveway, sat up, and pulled the hood of her sweatshirt down over her eyes. She sat like that until the police showed, their red and blue lights pulsing and dancing across the walls of our living room. I cracked the door and gave a statement to the police. After trying in vain to question the drunken girl, they loaded her into an ambulance and took her to detox.

After the police left I paced around the house for a while, watching snippets of *Northern Exposure*; but I was easily distracted. I couldn't help but think about how the situation might have been different. What if I'd forgotten to lock the door? What if she made it into the house? What if she'd been a man? What if she'd hurt herself?

Strangely enough I wasn't so worried about what *she* might have done. Instead what worried me—frightened me actually—was how quickly, coolly, and rationally I had decided that I could destroy anyone or anything that threatened my son. He was just two days old. I was just barely a father, still green. But some instinct clicked inside and I knew, as soon as I heard that doorknob rattling, that I could kill to protect him from harm.

Into the Mild

BLUE HOUSES

In the fall of 2002 I moved with my wife and our infant son into a blue house on the Cache le Poudre River outside of Fort Collins, Colorado.

Our son had been born the previous May and was already big, already crawling and close to walking, learning to explore the world. We lived in a tiny 800 square foot house and my office was the ottoman. At night I often slept on the floor, behind the easy chair, because I couldn't sleep with the baby in bed. I'm a light sleeper who usually needs the noise of a fan to fall asleep. In that house I felt cramped and confined, pressed into a tiny cage. We needed a change, needed more space. That's how I stumbled across an ad for the blue house.

The house, an old cabin converted into a two-bedroom rental, was painted sky-blue and perched above State Highway 14, 10 miles up the Poudre Canyon in the foothills of the Rocky Mountains. For the eight months or so that we lived there, we existed somewhere in the penumbra between civilization and wilderness, safety and danger, sanity and madness.

We moved to the hills away from the bright center of Fort Collins and our tiny house. We moved closer to the shadows of human life, and this new house—existing as it did in the margins—seemed like the kind of house we were supposed to want. We thought of ourselves as adventurous, nature-loving faux hippies who didn't need the traffic and noise and crime of the city. We should have loved it. We should have embraced the adventure together. We should have been happy.

A bright white deck skirted one side of the house and lurched out over the highway that ran just below our feet, just a sneeze away, between the house and the river. If you fell off the deck, there was a good chance you'd end up on the pavement. But standing on the deck, back from the edge, the highway was so close, you couldn't even see it. You just heard the cars growl past in the night. If you blocked out the noise, or stood out there early in the morning, you could pretend it was just the river rolling and tumbling past. In the fall the blonde hills were splashed with patches of purple undergrowth and the river turned a deep milky green.

Right away we had problems with the house. Somehow it looked different on the day we moved in—smaller, darker, danker, cold and empty. It had lots of brown wood paneling and an ancient death-trap propane heater that, when the heat came on, roared like a jet taking off.

There was a telling moment that day, one of those moments from which there is no return; we were carrying boxes up the steps and cramming our furniture inside. I lingered inside, unloading boxes in the fading light, watching the space fill fast. My wife came up the stairs and stepped through the door.

A look crossed her face. I watched her try to push it away, watched her try to suppress the rising darkness. I could see it all. An unmistakable distance settled over her, and I knew she was retreating before we'd even settled. I knew she'd already left and I felt like I was looking up at her from the bottom of the canyon.

We tried to make the best of it. We tried to appreciate the outdoors—often hiking around the foothills with our son in a backpack. And it was idyllic at times, peaceful and quiet. Mountains and canyons were our backyard, a river in the front. We both lost pounds by the dozen carrying the baby up and down trails, dragging the dog along with us. But the romance faded after a while and we settled in for a long winter.

As close as we were to the highway, we weren't too far from the wilderness and new kinds of danger—a rushing river or rolling fire. The house where we lived was, in fact, nearly wiped out by a huge wildfire in 2012. Most ghostly and psychologically troubling of all threats, though, were dun-colored pumas lurking in the undergrowth. Mountain lions. Big cats. This was something new, something I hadn't predicted. We might have moved out of the city but we'd also leaped into the lion's territory and moved into a lower status on the food chain.

The attack tales—people pounced upon, eaten, mauled, etc.—haunted me. I read the stories on the news and replayed the images over and over in my head, hoping it would help me protect my family. A ten-year-old boy, hiking with his family in Rocky Mountain National Park, runs ahead of the rest, around a bend in the trail, just doing what boys do. This is often how it starts. Seconds later the father comes upon a lion dragging the boy off into the brush.

I didn't want to live in fear. I knew the statistics. I read all about it. I knew that we had invaded their habitat. Not the other way around. And I knew that attacks were uncommon and fatal attacks even more rare. But as we moved in that first day, the landlord—a bleached-out tweaker, the wife of a local personal injury attorney, who liked to talk about herself a lot—felt the need to tell us about the scores of mountain lions roaming the hills, snatching pets from yards and terrorizing the humans. She made it seem like they were camped on the roof of our house, licking their chops, just waiting for a chance to pounce on our baby. We stood there in the driveway, my wife holding the baby on her hip, and I wanted to tell this woman to shut the hell up, to stop and think for a minute about what she was saying to her new tenants, new parents, new aliens to this country.

I admit that she scared us and, at first, we kept the dog inside or in the tiny fenced-in yard. I worried obsessively about the big cats when we were outside with our son and I hovered over him constantly. I was glad that he was still learning how to use his legs, still toddling around and mostly attached to one of us on such adventures. I didn't want him to be independent in the woods. I didn't want him striking out ahead of us around one of those bends. Not yet at least. Because you never knew when he might not come back.

DEFENSIVE STORYTELLING

On July 17, 1997, ten-year-old Mark David Miedema was hiking with his family in Rocky Mountain National Park, a couple of hours away from where I lived with my girlfriend in Breckenridge. The family had taken the North Inlet Trail to Cascade Falls on the west side of the park. The trail skirts the edge of Summerland Meadow, a popular feeding spot for deer and elk. On their way up to the falls that afternoon, Mark had sprinkled peanuts along the trail in his best Hansel and Gretel. As the family made their way back down the trail, Mark ran ahead of the group following his map of crumbs. He was only a few minutes away but far enough out of their sight that none of the adults could see what happened next.

At approximately 4:30 p.m. just at the edge of Summerland Meadow, Mark was attacked by an 88-pound mountain lion. He suffered bite and puncture wounds to his head, face, and neck; and evidence suggested that he fought off the attack, at least for a while. A lion will typically try to quickly break the neck or crush the skull of its prey. When the family came upon him, Mark's legs were protruding from a bush beside the trail. The lion had his head in her mouth and was trying to drag his body further off the path.

I'm just retelling what I read in different reports. You can read all of it online, or most of it at least. There are a number of sites that collect stories of fatal mountain lion and/or bear attacks and they are filled with dark little horrors of language clipped from news reports, sentences such as, "A cougar tore apart pieces of five-year-old Carmen Schrock's skull at a campground near Metaline Falls, Washington," and other snippets that are captivating in their detached, objective reporting of gruesome attacks, many of them on children, made even more disturbing by the listing catalogue form they use. I had a hard time looking away, not clicking links and chasing stories down rabbit holes. It was bad.

I lost whole hours, days even, to their morbid march of facts and information. I was pretty sure this made me a terrible person. I didn't know if my reading and retelling these stories is another kind of attack or an act of empathy. I hoped it was the latter, but some days as I combed through each story for the strange, grotesque, or odd details, I wondered if I wasn't just another kind of predator, hunting for the attack stories.

In fact, people who knew that I'd been interested in this stuff for a while would sometimes send me links to news reports of people being horrifically mauled by predators. There were a lot of them. In fact, if you paid attention, they seemed to be happening all the time, all around us. And I ate it all up.

When the lion that killed Mark Miedema was later tracked down, shot, and killed by a professional lion hunter, a necropsy showed that she was pregnant with two cubs. I had no idea what to think about this fact, in part because it seems too strange, too sublime and specific, to be true, and also because it seems like the stuff of story and not reality: the unpredictable and inevitable ending that we expect from great fiction.

We'd moved into a lions' den. We were tempting fate, homesteading in the penumbra, encroachers, trespassers, and we felt utterly alone in our pioneering. When we hiked around the forty acres we leased and in the county park across the river, I kept the dog on the leash and carried a large walking stick. I bought into the fear and the hype. I'd even found the bones, fur, and blood of a deer on the hillside behind our place and wondered if there was a big cat hunting up there.

One morning during our regular walk, the dog came trotting up to me with the forelimb of a deer in her mouth.

She dropped it at my feet and wagged her tail, and I thought, *this is fucking crazy*.

I imagined the cat perched on the rocky outcropping behind our bright blue house. He was the color of rocks and grass, invisible, the color of a ghost. His whiskers twitching in the breeze, he gazed down into our son's bedroom, watching him sleep, waiting for his chance.

I knew our chance of even seeing a mountain lion— much less being attacked by one—was pretty small; but still I found myself wondering why we had decided to risk the odds. At my most panicked moments, my imagination took over and sometimes it surprised me how detailed and violent my protective fantasies became:

> *It begins with a swift attack. The cat latches onto my son, but I am there in a split-second, punching wildly at the cat's face. He lets go and turns on me. I tell the boy to run. He is hurt and dazed but he gets away somehow, out of the scene, and I focus on the animal. He leaps at me, aiming for my throat and rakes me with his claws. He clamps his jaws down on my left arm. With my right hand, I press my thumb into the cat's eyeball as hard and deep as I can, until I feel membranes bursting and cells collapsing. The cat twists, snapping bones in my arm. He claws at my belly, but I keep thrusting, turning my thumb and pushing nail-down further and further into the eye until finally the cat releases its grip and bounds away, mewing and spitting, pawing at the damaged eye.*

I found myself engaging in these sorts of fantasies far too often. It was a strange sort of defensive imagining. In the end of them, of course, I always won. I always fought off the predator and protected my son. Thus are the narratives of fatherhood. Since fear is primarily psychological phenomena and danger often a matter of interpretation, I wondered if imagination, if storytelling and essaying, was the best defense I could put up for my family.

INTO THE HALF-WILD

A few years before we moved into Cache le Poudre Canyon, on October 2 1999, three-year-old Jaryd Atadero, hiking with a group of adults, disappeared in the Canyon without a trace. Bright-eyed and curious, he'd run ahead of the slow adults in his group, exploring the woods—engaging in the kind of mesmerized stomp into the brush I've seen other kids adopt.

Toddlers love the woods because it's so easy to get lost. Too easy perhaps. It feels safe, comforting, and distant from the obvious evils and dangers of civilization. The group of adults assumed Jaryd had joined the other group ahead, that he simply chose another circle of safety. But he didn't. He never made it to them. Nobody knows for sure what happened. He just disappeared. Massive search efforts, lasting days, weeks, months, turned up nothing. No evidence. No tracks. No signs of struggle. No blood. No nothing.

At least for a few years. Then they found him. Or parts of him.

On June 6, 2003, shortly after we'd moved out of the canyon, back to Fort Collins, Jaryd's scattered skeletal remains, his tattered red jacket, and his shoe were found. Some hikers discovered the remains, not far from the trail but well hidden in thick brush and rocks on a steep hillside, a place that would have been difficult for Jaryd to climb alone. Though it was nearly impossible to prove, pretty much everyone concluded that Jaryd had been attacked, killed and eaten by a mountain lion. They don't know when it happened or how long he was lost before he died.

It's a horrible story. But after a while of living in the same canyon where Jaryd had disappeared the part that really began to trouble me was not the part about the mountain lion acting like a mountain lion. That was bad and worried me plenty, especially with my son now getting more mobile, close to walking all on his own. The new fear that developed there related to another part of Jaryd's story, a part of the story that seemed to speak more to the nature of the half-wild, the mild penumbra in which we lived, and where Jaryd died, than any tale of a lion lurking in the brush.

When he was lost, perhaps before anyone had noticed, before they began searching, Jaryd stumbled across two fly-fishermen working a hole in a nearby creek close to the trailhead. These men, annoyed by his innocent noise, worried he would frighten the trout, shooed Jaryd away, telling him to be quiet and go back to his parents. They were fishing for chrissakes, and they had to be thinking, "Come on, where's this kid's parents? He's scaring away all the fish."

They were the last two people to see Jaryd alive.

The half-wild has a strange effect on your understanding of self and society. That little boy didn't belong there. But he wasn't really their responsibility. Not yet. After all, the trail wasn't far. There was a parking lot not too far away. His parents had to be nearby. Why else would he be there? It was a well-traveled path, popular with city folks who drive up for a day hike. They just needed to get him away from their fishing hole.

In the half-wild, where everyone goes to shed his social responsibilities, individualism is the norm. Survival is *your* responsibility. Deep in the wilderness, away from most trails, in what you might call the "backcountry," those fishermen would have most likely reacted differently. They would have been far enough away from civilization that their sense of collective duty to fellow human beings might have easily extended to a little lost boy. They probably would have protected him, fed him, kept him warm and searched for his parents.

But in the half-wild? What happens? There's an odd suspension, a dangerous dallying between the individual and the social, between right and wrong. This is no place for welfare, no home for the weak or those easily lost and dependent. People retreat to the half-wild to shed their responsibility to others. Most likely those fishermen weren't bad men. They meant no harm to the boy. But something had shifted out there, or at least in the managed wilderness of the Canyon. I suspected it was also true that if Jaryd had approached the same men on the street in downtown Fort Collins, wandering alone without his parents nearby, they would have reacted differently. They would have sheltered and protected him there too. At the very least, they would have taken the boy to the police station and helped him find safety.

In the half-wild, the mild, the in-between, the rules lose definition and boundaries.

They become hazy and porous, prone to collapse.

MAD WINDS

The wind was driving me mad. Channeled by the canyon's rock walls, the wind howled down the canyon and slammed into our house like a train gone off the rails. The whole place shook and the windows whistled until I duct-taped their seams. I had trouble sleeping for more than an hour at a time and was often pulled awake at 3 a.m. for no reason except the noise of my own thoughts. I started having panic attacks at work. I'd watch the weather, see the snow swirling in the air, and my heart would race and I'd feel on the verge of tears or screaming. It was hard for me to explain or control. I wasn't eating much, either. I called my doctor and she prescribed a pill that made me feel dumb and slow, incapable of caring about anything, including sex. I watched a lot of television and didn't write a thing. I pretended I liked it out there in the mild. Then the blizzard came. It was March 18, 2003, late enough that we thought we'd escaped the worst of winter in the canyon.

It dumped snow for two days as we squirreled away in the house with our son and watched it pile up. Ice formed on the inside of the windows and the wind whipped the snow into a thick meringue that completely buried our cars. The blue outlines of my pickup truck just kind of faded into the landscape. The snow blasted my wife's white Honda on one side, leaving the edges exposed and completely burying it on the other until it was nearly indistinguishable in the drifts.

Occasionally I would pull on my boots and venture out into the snow, post-holing my way around the back of the house, climb up on the roof, and make sure the exhaust vents for the gas stove and the water heater weren't clogged. I carried a broom and a shovel and tried to clear space around the vents and knock ice off the eaves. The wind pushed against me, throwing snow in my face. I stood there on the roof of our house and noticed how everything seemed poured over, flattened, blurred out, and the snow looked like it wanted to swallow our entire house.

When it stopped and the sun came out, there was close to four or five feet of snow in the Canyon, and at least three feet in most parts of Fort Collins. We lost power and phone service for a while. Our furnace was propane, so we still had heat. But our water was well-water pumped by electricity; so we soon ran out. We watched the news and saw that the whole Front Range had been hit hard and that the weight of the snow had brought down trees all over Fort Collins and collapsed roofs of homes and businesses. It would end up being one of the biggest and costliest storms to ever hit the Front Range of Colorado.

In the Canyon snowplows cleared the highway within a few hours after the storm passed and the spring sun did the rest of the work, leaving the road easily passable. They did nothing, however, for my driveway. I stood out on the deck, watching other cars pass on the road, and tried to figure out how I was going to get my family out of there, back to civilization. I soon began to itch at the feeling of being trapped. I didn't like to feel trapped. My skin felt too small, tight and constricting like a shirt that no longer fit. I had to do something. The panic was rising like a tide. We were stuck.

I started at the back of my wife's Honda. The snow was so deep I had to shovel in layers, taking the top few inches off first and moving methodically down. I could only work for about a half-hour at a time before I needed a break. My shoulders ached, my back throbbed and my legs felt weak. But I didn't want to be trapped in that house any longer. I couldn't quit. I couldn't sit still, couldn't be much of a father or a husband, couldn't enjoy any of it. I wanted out. Out of the snow, out of the canyon, out of the mild, out of this dark hole I'd fallen into there.

My son rumbled around the house and bounced in his plastic bouncy-chair. My wife used the cell phone to contact people, or try to contact people; but mostly she just spent the time playing with our son, not panicking. I wasn't so good at the not-panicking. Instead I shoveled for at least four hours until I had cleared about 1000 cubic feet of snow and opened a path from our house down to the highway.

Not knowing where we were going or what we intended to do, but just needing to get out of the blue house, the three of us packed into our Trooper and drove into town. As soon as we reached the city limits, we saw how bad it was there. Trees laden with spring growth had collapsed under the weight of snow and the town looked like it had been hit with a tornado and a blizzard. The streets were furrowed with huge ridges of snow, some of them blocked off completely and impassable. I feel guilty now for admitting this, but it made me happy to see this.

Out there in the canyon I started to feel like we were being punished, and it was good for us to see that the town had been hit hard too, that we were not alone. It was comforting to know that other people were dealing with the same challenges. We'd begun to feel isolated from normal human life, and it had a way of coloring our view of the world.

Many of the streets in town had not been plowed and it was clear that people were stranded in their homes just as we had been. They were lucky if they were close enough to a major street that had been plowed that they could park a car and walk. Most people couldn't leave, couldn't escape, even if they'd shoveled for four hours as I did.

They couldn't leave—but they had each other. They were not isolated in their homes. Neighbors talked with neighbors. People could stand on their porches and say, "Wow," together and not be afraid, not worry about the streets and their driveway or survival. Out there in the canyon, in the midst of the mild I'd felt utterly alone, close to community but not close enough for it to matter.

We felt safe in Fort Collins, even if we didn't have electricity, because we had friends and some sense of community. Living in the canyon had begun to feel like living in something vastly deeper than an intellectual, emotional, and pyschological rut; and it felt good to be back in town, hunkering down with friends, waiting in peace for the snow to melt. We spent the night drinking and cooking on the gas stove by candlelight or flashlight; we played board games and talked and laughed and never felt alone or isolated or afraid.

INTO THE DARKNESS

Sometime after 1:30 a.m. on January 18, 2003, on a suburban street in Fort Collins, a twenty-year-old young woman named Lacy Miller was driving home alone after an evening out with friends. The next morning, her mother would find Lacy's car parked on the street nearby, just two doors down. The car doors had been locked and the vehicle showed no signs of foul play.

Though nobody knew it at the time, a black Ford Explorer with a blue dashboard-light had pulled over Lacy's car in the Quail Hollow neighborhood where her parents lived. A young man wearing dark clothes and a badge on a chain around his neck climbed out of the Explorer and approached Lacy's car. He shined a flashlight in her face, accused her of driving drunk, demanded her license, and ordered her out of the car. Then he handcuffed her, and put her into his vehicle.

The young man with the badge and the blue light was not a police officer, though. He wasn't really a man at all. His name was Jason Peder Clausen, a local kid, the average son of average parents, just a boy who'd always wanted to become a police officer. Clausen had even participated in a kind of Junior Law Officer training program; and not long before Lacy's disappearance, Clausen went online and purchased a blue dashboard light and a badge on a chain.

Clausen knew how cops acted, how they looked and talked, and he knew how susceptible people were to authority, particularly an underage young woman driving home after having a drink or two, a perfectly innocent person, a good girl who followed the rules and respected authority. He knew these people were the easiest to intimidate. He knew how to bully people. He'd flipped on that light, draped a badge around his neck and donned a blue POLICE baseball cap. Clausen handcuffed Lacy and stuffed her in his car.

Lacy must have realized something was wrong. But when? When did the scales fall away and the truth get revealed? When did she know that Clausen's authority was all image and lies? The details were fuzzy. We didn't know much for certain. We knew that Clausen was tweaking on meth, and had been for days. He confessed to everything, though there were details he couldn't recall clearly or didn't want to recall.

We know that he took Lacy to his house that night, sneaked her past several roommates into his bedroom, where he beat and raped her; and, at some point, he killed her, wrapped her body in a plastic tarp and put it in the backseat of his SUV. The next day he asked his roommate to help him move something in his car and showed him Lacy's body. And though it took him a couple of days to come forward, the roommate knew at that moment that this was the girl for whom everyone was searching, the girl whose picture he'd seen on the news and in the papers.

Clausen loaded Lacy's body on a trailer, covered it with construction materials, hitched it to his car, and drove it up the Poudre Canyon, past our blue house, to an area just off the main highway, about a mile from us, same side of the road. The place was a spot where Clausen used to retreat on the weekends with friends to drink and shoot guns, a kind of liminal space between roads. He dragged the girl's body up into the trees and tried to burn it with lighter fluid and the few scattered bits of wood he could find. When that failed, he buried her in a pile of dirt.

I knew when they'd found Lacy. Eight days after she disappeared, I sat on the deck of the blue house and watched the stream of ambulances and police cars flowing up the Canyon. It had to be her, I thought. This was more than a drowning in the river, more than a car accident. There were plenty of those in the Canyon too. All the time, really. But this time, the city cops came. That never happens.

I'd been watching the news, reading the reports in the papers. I thought about the girl's mother. I'd seen her on television trying to be stoic and resolute in her belief that they would find her daughter; and I thought about the anger she must have felt at some point—not so much at the boy (which was part of it of course) but at the world for allowing these sorts of things to happen, perhaps at this half-wild place we called home for being the place where her daughter was buried. At this point, I did not yet have a daughter, but I had a son and, watching that mother on television, reading her words in the paper, I felt angry, too. I felt disillusioned and frustrated and I knew we had to get out of the Canyon.

I read the news stories obsessively, compulsively, and selfishly I thought about the fact that the place where we had moved with our young child—this gray zone between city and wild—was where a sick kid, twisted on meth, pretending to be a police officer, believed he could hide and desecrate the life of an innocent girl, a place where people seemed to die and disappear at alarming rates, in especially gruesome ways—or at least in ways that captivated and shocked the collective psyche of an extended community. I didn't want to be part of another shocking and tragic story. I knew bad things happened all over the place, quietly, subversively, but it felt like we were circling closer to danger and I just wanted to stop the spin for a while.

At some point, I got it. I learned my lesson. I believe that nature, even managed and packaged nature, has the potential as a lens to reveal both the best and worst of people, to strip away the layers of protection and pretension and lay bare one's internal workings. And I knew that somewhere in that Canyon, in those penumbral foothills between deep wilderness and civilization, in the midst of the half-wild, some of us could become dangerously unmoored. I think I had begun to lose sight of the best of myself, and I was afraid of what it could do to my son and to our family. I had a vision of myself, drugged out on anti-anxiety meds, unable to write or to feel anything fully, cocooned safely inside our blue house, the blue light of the television glowing on my face, my veins coursing with sluggish blood. I'd never be troubled by the Canyon again, never be troubled by anything. The vision was terrifying. And I knew we had to leave, had to escape the steep horizons and narrow strip of sky that shaped our life in the Canyon.

To a lot of people, the Poudre Canyon was a place of security and peace, of much-needed calm and moments of meditation. It is a truly beautiful place. I felt some of that peace. I did. We all did. Or we tried. Happiness visited like a hummingbird visits a feeder, giving us just a taste before hovering for a second, just out of reach, and then disappearing altogether in a blur of color. For me the canyon was much deeper and darker than I could have expected; and though I feel like a failure admitting it here now on the page, it was good to leave the Poudre River canyon and return to a city laid out in a predictable grid, where our mistakes and horizons didn't loom overhead, jagged and steep, but seemed to spread out before us, unfurling like a map webbed with possible paths to different, brighter destinations.

Bright Orange Fear

TOUCHING THE NEST

To my two-year-old son, born into a post 9/11 world, the recent elevation of the terrorism threat-level to orange did not mean much. Orange did not make him more vigilant at the mall with his mom. Orange did not inspire xenophobia at the park or fervent patriotism at Donna's Daycare. It did not cause him to seal himself in his room with plastic tarps and duct tape, secluded away with his stuffed dog, Bob, and a five gallon jug of apple juice.

Orange was simply a color.

Orange for him was the color of joy and comfort, not the terror alerts or a prisoner's jumpsuit. One of the highest compliments he paid was to call me "Orange Daddy." It's the color of fruit, juice, gum and his old exer-saucer bouncy chair. It's the color of safety and playground equipment, popsicles and plastic balls, shovels and buckets. Orange was his windbreaker jacket, the Faraway Park, the curly slide, a butterfly, and a hot air balloon. Orange was the color of sunsets, fireworks, and a choo-choo train.

Orange was not the color of fear; or it *shouldn't* have been.

The radio told us every morning that we were under a terror alert. Buildings had been barricaded in New York, bolted, and sandbagged for safety. Black helmeted riot police were posted. I still wasn't sure what orange meant. I sat at my desk in my home office in Colorado and thought about the color of things in the larger world and how to explain them to my son. I thought about what stories to tell him, what lessons from the past I could impart to ensure a safe future—and in this I was eternally caught between time.

Outside my window, a yellow-jacket buzzed in and out of a small hole in the white siding. My son knew about yellow-jackets already. He knew to respect them. I told him, "If you don't bother them, they won't bother you."

He was curious about the threat. He wanted to understand them; and I wanted to teach him. Unlike his little sister who is terrified of bugs, he liked the yellow-jackets' colors and the noise they made. One day he stood in the green grass watching them and he pointed at the hole in the siding. He told me, "See dat black hole, Daddy. Dat's where the nest lives." Then he knitted his brow and lowered his eyes like he'd seen me do when I tried to act serious. He was mimicking my concern.

"We don't touch the nest," he said. "It's dangerous."

TARGETED

Having left the foothills, we lived again in Fort Collins, the Front Range of the Rocky Mountains, surrounded by military bases, oil refineries, missile silos, defense contractors, and toxic waste sites; in other words, surrounded by targets—the sorts of sites the government tells us terrorists will be striking next.

Our neighborhood seemed safe enough. We didn't *feel* like we're in danger. But fear still found its way into our reality, seeped in like black water under the door—the first suggestion of a leak; possibly a flood of fear—and I didn't know how to plug it back up again.

One day the sun was baking our yard, turning the green grass a dull grayish-brown in spots and leaving the blades brittle and crunchy underfoot. The sky appeared a ridiculous shade of blue—artificially rich and deep and alive. My wife worked in the yard, watering the flowers and trees and grass, trying to save them from the sun, and just playing with the hose. I watched my son, naked and soaking wet, cram his finger into the hose, making a long arc of water that doused my wife. She screamed and ran. My son squealed with delight. He was having so much fun.

I wished I could be outside with them, but I felt sick with a summer cold, fighting a fever. Throughout the day I'd been slipping in and out of sweaty sleep. Everything sort of shimmered and buzzed in my brain. Bright colors hurt. So did loud noises. I watched them for a while until I felt lightheaded and had to retreat back to bed.

I'd lain down for a few minutes when suddenly the front door burst open. My wife stormed into the house with our son on her hip. She yelled, "Steve! Steve! Where's the phone?" and our son was crying, clearly confused and frightened. My brain hurt. I sat up in bed. Our son toddled into the room and I picked him up.

"What's going on?" I asked.

Our son laid his head on my shoulder as his mother frantically searched for the phone. She wrote a number down on a piece of paper.

"I have to call the police," she said as she grabbed the phone and dialed 911.

I held the boy in my lap and heard her tell the police what she'd seen. I heard it at the same time they did.

I was standing in my front yard with my son and I heard this noise, a loud noise, and I looked up, and I see this car, a brownish Honda Accord, parked on the street in front of the neighbor's house and there's a guy standing behind the car and the trunk is open and he's got his hand on the trunk and he's screaming something and there's a woman lying in the trunk and he slams the trunk, gets in the driver's seat, and takes off.

(pause)
Yes, I'm sure it was a woman. I saw her jeans, her tank-top, and her long hair. She was curled up in the trunk.

(pause)
Dark. It was dark hair. Brunette, I think. Maybe black. But I saw skin. I saw her skin, like her shoulder or something.

(pause)
Yes, I've got the license number right here.

She read them the license number, gave our address, and a few minutes later, two police cars pulled up in front of the house. My wife patiently told her story all over again to the patrol officers, retelling several details, recreating the scene just to be as clear as possible. She tried to be convincing, tried to make it real. The police officers knocked on doors and interviewed all the neighbors they could find, asking questions, trying to find out if anyone saw the car or knew the people in the car, but nobody saw much of anything.

"Are you sure it was a brown Accord?" they asked her again.

"Yes, I'm sure. Sort of a light brownish gold color," she said.

The guy next door said he saw the car parked there an hour earlier but didn't see anyone inside. We waited in the house while the officers made their rounds, asking more questions and leaving notes on doors.

My wife filled out a witness statement form, writing out the whole thing again, cementing the truth of it in her mind. She told them what the guy was wearing, the color of his hair, and a rough estimate of his height. When the officers came back, they told us that they had five squad cars out searching for the brown Accord. They'd tracked down the license and now had a name. They said they'd let us know if and when they find out what was going on. They thanked her for keeping her eyes open and being a concerned citizen. They rehashed a couple of details from her statement—hair color, car color, clothes, height—and then they left us with our imaginations and this new story of our neighborhood, our town, our world. We were left with memory and fear. We were left with words like *what if, maybe, rape, dead* and more we could barely utter. The words, the images, the possibilities just sort of hung around the house, the whole day, like a pervasive stink. After this, things just looked different—sort of waxy, muted, and soft, barely real at all.

THE GIFT

The red brick house where we lived backed up to a city park. Kids played soccer there on the weekends while their parents screamed at them. The park had a swing-set, a big red plastic swing, a sandbox, teeter-totter, a creek and a playground—a faded pink playground—and I always thought our son was lucky to have these things in his backyard, so close to his nest. We now live in a place with few parks and school playgrounds that aren't fenced off and locked, so we put a wooden playground in the backyard. It has a climbing wall and a slide and three swings; and because it is made of wood, and because it's already a little battered and rickety, it reminds me of the playgrounds of my youth, where so many lessons and dramas were played out.

Playgrounds now are all covered in soft, safe, bright and happy plastic. You can spot them miles away. Indeed, if we ever visit a new city and need something to occupy the children or a place to pic-nic, we just drive around, looking for the tell-tale beacon of bright yellow plastic. But these are not the playgrounds of my youth. The rope bridges aren't dangerous at all. The play structures are sanitized, rubberized, colorized and lobotomized. Some now are even surrounded by a blanket of cedar chips, making the playground look more like a hamster cage than a place for human children.

How exactly do you build a cedar-chip castle anyway?

Why does it all have to be so brightly colored?

I realize that they're safer now and that fewer children are injured or maimed by playground equipment. I realize that you could argue this is something good insurance companies have done for our kids. But I still don't like them. They shimmer and glow obscenely amidst green grass and trees. They scream orange safety. Danger is supposed to be a distant dream in the play areas of my children's generation; and I think this is mostly a good thing.

I hear the warnings of increased threats to my security, my family's security—and I think that maybe they're just messing with my head; maybe the real threat is all these vague warnings oozing out from the televisions and radios. Maybe the real threat is the distraction from danger in our own neighborhoods. They want us to see or hear "orange" and think: *Increased vigilance. Tightened security. Threats all around. Bag checks. Men with guns or box-*

butters or beards. Fear. Fear. FEAR. It's all about fear. But what about brown Accords? What about the rattle of a doorknob at 3:00 in the morning? What about right outside our doors?

The way I've always seen it, fear is a product of an active imagination. It's a feeling you get when the images in your head, the reality you create in your mind feels just a little too real, a little too possible. It's not necessarily a bad thing. I like to think of fear as a gift of the imagination—a wild, unruly and powerful gift.

I tell myself that if I can teach my son how to harness the gift, he will be a more confident, more mature individual. This would mean, of course, that fear, even danger, is actually something within my control; and just when I feel confident that this might be true, someone tries to claim my fear, tries to own it for their own reasons. Someone reminds me that my son isn't safe in the world. Someone pushes all my buttons.

TRACKING FEAR

Mondays are father-son days. Much of this time is spent in public parks and playgrounds. We visit green plastic playgrounds and red plastic playgrounds. There are pink ones and orange ones; and this is how my kids often know them. My son always liked the red playground. It was more fun than green. It had red ladders and a curly-slide. Red was fun. Red was for the big kids. In the place where we live now, the Central Valley of California, a place some people call the "new Appalachia," the message of safety broadcast by colored plastic playgrounds is often overwritten with graffiti tags, marks of ownership and territory.

I understand that the blacktop road in front of

our house is statistically more dangerous than anything we'll likely find at a public park; but I also understand that danger is a matter of probability, reason, logic, and mathematical certainty, while fear is a matter of the heart or the gut or some other part of the brain.

Fear is fundamentally irrational, an amalgam of emotion and experience, an offspring of the imagination, that does not always correspond to the statistical reality of danger. Thus when your choices are motivated by the gift of fear, it's really tough to explain the reasons. That's when we make the mistake of believing that because we are afraid then the danger must be real.

This is a lesson I'm learning all over again as a parent. Just because I'm afraid that my kids will be abducted by some sicko, drown in the city pool, or be blown up in an airplane—just because my imagination works overtime inventing danger—doesn't mean that the danger actually exists.

Or does it?

One Monday morning during our regular father-son trip to a park in Fort Collins, my son and I were walking along the river, chucking rocks in the clear water. We sat on the green banks for almost a half-hour watching a crew of men with chainsaws and a yellow backhoe tractor cut through underbrush and load it into a red dump truck. On the way back to the car, we stopped at the playground and my son made his way between the different slides and such, moving from one thing to the next in fluid motion. He felt the rhythms of this landscape.

I watched him climb the red ladder on the pink playground and do the curly slide and then I spotted this guy, a stranger, walking around the perimeter of the sand. Most days it's just the two of us here, sometimes a random mother and child, rarely another father and son. You *never* see a single guy at the playground here. It just doesn't happen here.

I began to catalog details—the kind of stuff you'd need for an eyewitness report. He wore a green cloth Panama-style hat with the salty white sweat-stains of someone who works outside in the sun. He wore gray shorts, a black fleece vest, and brown hiking boots. His legs were stocky like those of a rugby player or a mailman. He carried a long skinny stick or pointer of some kind. He held it up near his chin, sighted down it, and kind of wiggled it around just above the ground as he walked. At first I thought he was just crazy, maybe a homeless guy with some ghosts. There were a couple of times I thought I caught him looking at my son and my Spidey-sense tingled.

I have no doubt of the protective wrath I could unleash if I felt my son was in danger. I'm 6'4" and weigh over 250 lbs. I literally envision myself as a sow grizzly protecting her cub, swatting at danger with my massive paws and just generally going ape-shit crazy on anyone who threatened him. I promise you they'd need a tranquilizer gun and some kind of large net to bring me down. They could relocate me to a distant mountain valley and I'd find my way back to gnaw on the skull of anyone who laid a hand on my son. The incident with the drunken girl on our porch confirmed this for me.

This guy just walked around the playground equipment staring at the ground and kind of pointing that stick. He didn't make eye-contact with me and moved very slowly and deliberately, as if he was lost in his own thoughts. I watched him vigilantly for a while. Pretty soon, though, I got distracted and took my eye off the guy.

My boy rambled around in the sand, climbing the equipment, chirping and squealing. He involved me in a game of hide-and-seek, and I dropped my guard for a few moments. I ignored my fear instinct, let my imagination lapse. I was hung up on the ladder as he zipped down the curly slide.

Suddenly the guy in the hat stood there waiting for him, just a few feet away from my son, closer to him now. He held a camera. He was going to take his picture. I hurried over, not sure what was happening, my hackles raised, my claws extended. I felt a growl building in my chest. I was ready to attack. My son looked up at him and the guy turned to me.

He smiled and stuck out his hand.

I hesitated for a moment then noticed the patch on his hat seemed to be some kind of insignia or badge. He introduced himself and explained that he was teaching a tracking class there tomorrow for the Larimer County Search and Rescue and they were working on a lost-child scenario.

"Tracking?" I asked.

"That's right," he said and pointed the stick at all the tracks in the sand.

He asked if he could take a picture of Malcolm's shoeprint, so I held my son's little foot up for the camera. He snapped the digital photo and turned it around to show us. He said to me, "You're the hiking boot, right?" as he traced some invisible path in the sand. I looked around the playground and saw a shifting pockmarked lunar-like surface of craters and prints. It seemed impossible that anyone could pick the tracks of a single person out of this mess.

The guy said, "I've tracked your son around the sand. He'll be our missing child tomorrow. Can you do me favor, though, and exit the playground over there and then walk towards the river?"

I told him that's no problem and the guy drifted

away as quietly as he'd arrived. My son played around a few more minutes and I walked him out the other side of the playground and through the high green grass toward the water—realizing briefly, sort of peripherally, that I'd just inserted my own son into a narrative about a missing boy who wandered off the playground and may have fallen into the river or been snatched. His shoe-print would be their clue and they would track him around the playground. They would study this shifting surface and follow his tracks.

They'd do everything they could to find my missing boy and, for this, I was deeply grateful. I was happy that we could play some small part in training Search and Rescue people to find lost children. But part of me wished I had never let that man take a picture of my son's foot. I understand and respect the power of stories. I know how they can color your world. I know what their magic can conjure.

In some imagined reality, my son would be missing; and as the idea settled into my consciousness, I didn't like the thought at all. I imagined ten or twelve students at this class, all of them looking at that picture and thinking about my son lost somewhere. I didn't like to mess with the creative power of narrative, or the very real fear it spawned in my gut. What is real after all? I felt guilty for toying with fate, as if I'd tempted the gods or spirits or the earth to take my boy from me. It hurt to even think about it. I felt like I had failed in my duties as a father.

THE CANYONS OF MANHATTAN

Two months before the brown Accord changed our view of home; my wife and I traveled to New York City without our son. It was her first time away from him for more than a night. We visited the Metropolitan Museum of Art and, among many other things, we saw sketches of a new project planned by Christo, the conceptual artist known for wrapping buildings in cloth and color and stringing up miles of giant killer umbrellas.

Christo planned to frame Central Park walkways with huge orange textile "gates." I looked at some of the preliminary sketches for the project and couldn't help but imagine what it would be like to stroll beneath a mad flapping tunnel of orange—those gates curling and snapping in the breeze—and the beauty of it stayed with me for a while, burning at the edges of my vision.

As we left the museum and drifted back out into the masses of people and traffic and noise, I resented the government's appropriation of color. I wanted to wander through gates of orange, wanted to picture this in the park, but inevitably found myself feeling sort of disembodied and anxious, thinking of terror and terrorists and this stupid war. We crossed the street, dodging flashes of yellow traffic amidst the black canyons of steel and glass and concrete, leaving the color orange behind.

My wife and I both agreed that it was strange to be in New York without our son. The city felt like a world away from Colorado—an island of shiny right-angle canyons with a natural bounty of neon and noise and pizza. I enjoyed the stimulation, the vitality, and the release from responsibility. Without our son, I didn't worry about crossing streets or losing sight of him in a store. It was freeing in some ways—this disembodied feeling—and painful in others. I felt like I'd had a limb amputated or a vital organ removed. I just didn't feel quite whole. This is how I always feel when I'm away from my kids.

Despite recent warnings and orange alerts, despite the fact that we were staying in an apartment just a block away from Ground Zero, I didn't feel like a target in New York. The only fear I felt was more a matter of anxiety at being away from our son—as if I'd left not my wallet behind, but my bleeding heart sitting on a table, and I was just operating with an artificial pump. The hard part was knowing I couldn't protect him if he was targeted.

At that age our children are hairless apes, fragile primate babies—really more brain than body, an intelligent bag of skin and bones. At the age of two, their fine motor skills are still sputtering, but both my kids were already playing language games, making jokes, and speaking in metaphors.

But if you'd dropped him in the mountains alone, or in the canyons of New York City, they'd be lucky to survive the night. In many ways they are wholly incapable of protecting themselves. They are innocent and helpless. That's part of what defines them as children and what defines my life now as a parent. I'm responsible for protecting this innocence and helplessness but also for teaching my children how to leave it behind.

THINGS LIKE THIS DON'T HAPPEN HERE

In our neighborhood in Fort Collins, a place regularly ranked in Money Magazine's top 10 places to live, we also had a vigilant widow. Two of them, in fact. Each of them trained an eye or two out their window at all times. They never missed a thing. When a new crew of college kids moved in, one of them showed up the first week with fresh-baked muffins and pamphlets from the city about how to be a good neighbor.

In our neighborhood, we don't have a lot of families like us, young couples with children—the sort of stuff you see in billboard advertisements for subdivisions with names like Harlan Ranch or Poet's Crossing. And there's been a pack of kids from two different houses who all hang out together, apparently unsupervised, often a little noisy, but relatively harmless and generally very sweet. Ours isn't the nicest block in town, but it's not the worst; even the worst neighborhood in Fort Collins probably wasn't a place you'd need to be afraid to walk at night.

People always talked about how "safe" Fort Collins was, about how they felt comfortable and worry-free. Many people move to the Front Range from large cities on the East Coast just for the small-town feel of security. I knew lots of local residents who deliberately leave their doors unlocked at all times, and I always got the feeling that they did this to make a point, as a way of claiming some kind of ownership over fear.

They always told you about it, "Oh, I never lock the front door," as if this was supposed to impress me. It always seemed like they were trying to show off or display the trust they had in the community. It's not as if the physical action of locking a door and carrying a key was so unbelievably taxing that a normal person couldn't handle it, so clearly it was a more symbolic *inaction* than anything else. It was a symbolic rejection of fear, as if they can decide that they're safe and that's enough.

Of course the truth didn't always match the perception. We were not immune from crime. We are not always safe. But the image was powerful. We worked hard to maintain it. Even when our community was stalked by a serial rapist and countless police and news organizations warned people to lock doors and windows at night, you still saw quotes in the paper from people saying how they didn't want to "feel like a prisoner in their own home" or how it was "too hot to keep the screen door closed."

I got so sick and tired of hearing, "Things like this don't happen here," when quite obviously things like this were happening in our community—repeatedly. The danger was real but we didn't want to imagine it, so we ignored it.

A MATTER OF CHOICE

We couldn't ignore the brown Accord on that hot summer day in Fort Collins and how it altered the image of our neighborhood. We couldn't ignore the woman in the trunk, the suspense of waiting, the hazy colors of reality, and our electric imaginations fibrillating with possibilities.

Three hours after the police left, my fever still spiked up and down. I'd slept a little, but not much. My wife was a mess, too. Pretty much the whole time, she waffled between confidence and second-guessing herself, wondering one minute if she just imagined what she saw and being convinced the next that it was real or true (or whatever the opposite of imagined would be). She went over the details in her head again and again, trying to think of other explanations, trying to tell herself that perhaps that wasn't hair she'd seen, not flesh at all, maybe just some clothes stuffed in the trunk of that car. But why was the driver yelling? Why did he tear out of there so fast?

I tried to reassure her that the explanation was probably completely innocent and simple. But she really had no choice but to trust her instincts, no choice but to believe the truth of her perception. The hard part in this was that, on one level, she wanted to believe that she saw exactly what she thought she saw; but on another level she wanted to be completely deluded and wrong because the truth of her memory was an ugly painful truth that none of us wanted to face. She wanted to be right and she hoped she was wrong. We both did.

It was after 7:00 at night when the police finally knocked on the door again. I saw their cars parked out on the street and my heart raced, revving up like an engine. My brain was still cooking a bit from the fever. We all opened the door together. Our son stood between us and looked out the screen door. We watched them come and we waited for the truth and—in my imagination—it seemed it could go either way:

A: the first officer's face is set in a grim line, her brow furrowed. Her shoulders are sort of folded inward and she still hasn't looked up at our house, still hasn't acknowledged us. The second officer follows behind, staring at her partner's heels. She steps up on the porch and before she's even made eye contact, she begins apologizing and I know right away that this isn't going to be good. I know right away that my wife was right.

B: the first officer's face is relaxed. She walks side-by-side with her partner. She says something to her partner as they stroll casually up the driveway and they both smile. She looks up at us and says, "Hi," and sort of waves, and I know right away that everything is okay. I know right away that my wife was right.

Of course she was right. But the story was wrong. *B* is the answer.

140

They stopped the brown Honda and found it filled with teenagers. They asked to see in the trunk and found two girls who had volunteered to ride there because there wasn't room for them up front.

It was that simple. Public transportation. Nobody kept against her will. No dead bodies. No rape victims or sex slaves. Just a stupid choice in transportation. We apologized for wasting their time but the officers told us that we did the right thing, that we did exactly what we should have done. It was *their* job to find out the truth of *her* memory. They made that point very clear.

Of course I was preoccupied with the "what if" questions here. I wondered how we might have felt if they never found the car, if the police never showed up at our house that night and simply called from the station to tell us that they were working on the case but they didn't have any leads. How would this have changed our understanding of what my wife witnessed? Would we have convinced ourselves that it was innocent or horrible? I wonder how it might have changed the way we looked at our neighborhood or every single brown Honda Accord on the road. What would be the truth of this moment and how would it have colored our understanding of the world? It's almost impossible for me to imagine.

I learned that when it comes to fear and danger, we should trust our instincts but not our perceptions. We should believe our eyes, but know that things aren't always as they appear. How do you explain this to a child? How do I understand this myself? What is fear made of? How do I control it, contain it, and channel it? There is no rhyme for orange, no music or math to fear. Language can't even make sense of it for me. Colors confuse me. And I worry that I'll never be able to make sense of things for my children.

One day not long after the incident with the brown Accord, I picked our son up from Donna's Daycare. It was warm and sunny and he stood in the driveway waving when I pulled up. I loaded him in the car, buckled him into his safety seat, and we said, "Bye-bye" to Donna. As we pulled into traffic, I heard a report about an American hostage in Iraq—a man with a family in Georgia who I'd seen a picture of on the news earlier that day. He'd worn an orange jumpsuit and looked frightened. The radio report confirmed that, as promised by his black-hooded captors, he was beheaded with a sword.

Thankfully our son was chattering and singing and blissfully ignoring the news. Then he said, "I saw the guy wif the blue mouth, Daddy," and I just sort of let it go as I focused my attention back on the news, trying to imagine the horror and gore of a decapitation, resisting my morbid urge to see the video footage. Later at home he said again, "The guy wif the blue mouth is a little bit scary, Daddy" and this time I paid attention.

"What guy with the blue mouth?" I quizzed him.

"The guy," he said and paused for moment, "wif the blue mouth. Is he scary, Daddy?"

"No, he's not scary," I said, but this wasn't completely true. By now, he *was* a little bit scary to me. I couldn't stop the images welling up. Something was happening to me. I couldn't control it. Who was this guy? Where did he come from? The fear bubbled up more from my gut than my brain, spawned from whatever gland secretes it. I imagined some blue-teethed demon rattling the door lock, a blue-lipped pedophile with his face pressed against the window, maybe a monster with a big blue mouth leering at the children from his car.

"Did you see him at Donna's?" I asked.

"Uh huh," he said. "He's not scary, Daddy."

"Nope," I said. "He's silly." I tried to be calm and collected. I didn't even know for sure what we were talking about.

"He's silly?" my boy asked.

He seemed to need me to tell him this guy wasn't scary. He needed me to put aside *my* imagined reality and reassure him that he didn't need to be afraid. This looked like one of those important duties that parents perform.

This I could handle.

"Yep," I said. "He's just a silly blue-mouth guy. There's nothing to be afraid of."

That evening as we walked back from playing at the pink plastic playground, my son asked if he could see the sunset. From the park you get a perfect view of Horsetooth Rock, high above the reservoir of the same name, and the first rise of the Rocky Mountains. I hoisted him up on my shoulders as the sun began to slip down behind the black ridge of rock. The western horizon seemed to rise up from the earth and loom over us.

He pointed to the sky and said, "Look at those orange clouds, Daddy. They're pretty."

He was right. They were bright orange and beautiful and it was that simple.

The Colossal Colon

One day at a suburban mall in Rhode Island, my three-year-old son and I crawled through a giant disease-ridden colon. It was forty feet long, pink, and riddled with various forms of cancer. At the puckered entrance a smiling nurse asked us to don a pair of blue sanitary paper booties.

"Put these on your feet," she said. "It's to protect the colon."

I took the booties and resisted my juvenile urge to request some personal lubricant. This didn't seem like the way a dad should act around his son. I knew I should be more mature, be a better image of fatherhood, a role model or something; but we *were* about to crawl through something called the *Colossal Colon*. Etiquette seemed a dubious expectation at best. I wasn't sure there was a proper way to behave in a giant diseased intestine. Still, for the sake of my son, I suppressed my inner child and entered the colon.

I knew this experience was *supposed* to be educational and informative, and that my son could maybe even learn important lessons from it about health and his body. But what if it was just a toy, a playground accessory at the mall? As I ducked down to follow my son into the tunnel, I figured anything could happen.

That morning I'd read a story in the newspaper about the *Colossal Colon* touring exhibit designed to raise awareness about colorectal cancer and when I read the words, "40 foot long colon," I immediately knew that we had to see it. I don't know if other fathers had the same reaction, but it seemed like an opportunity I couldn't pass up—the sort of experience fathers and sons are supposed to share. The next step was to convince my son. With a toddler, the key to acquiescence is a successful sales pitch.

I presented it in this way, "Hey buddy, you wanna go to the mall and crawl through a giant pink tunnel?"

He answered predictably, "Can we, can we? Please!"

The *Colossal Colon's* visit to the mall happened to coincide with Potty Training Week for my son. He would start pre-school soon, and a recent email warned that our children must be 100% potty-trained—no exceptions. It included vague warnings about possible expulsion if our children could not master this skill (yes, I've learned that it is, indeed, a *skill* that must be *learned* and you can, in fact, be expelled from preschool for pooping issues). The pressure was on. So as a way to demystify the whole process of pooping, we'd been showing him pictures of the intestines in his "Body Book," and talking about the systems of his body, focusing most of our attention on the digestive system; and now we had the opportunity to take a tour of a giant pink colon.

Things were working out better than I'd imagined.

I explained on the drive to the mall that, while the colon does indeed play an important role in pooping, we couldn't really talk a lot about poop while we were in the mall.

"It's not polite to talk about that in public," I said as we parked the car.

We strolled up to the entrance with a mother and her three quiet well-behaved kids, and with her I exchanged the knowing sympathetic smile that parents give each other in public.

I doubted if she and her kids were there to see the

Colossal Colon.

Just as we approached the mall entrance, step-in-step with the mom and her kids, my son turned to me and asked, "Daddy, why can we not talk about poop at the *Colossal Colon*?"

I smiled at the woman and her kids, ignoring the horrified look on her face, and tried to distract my son from his current line of questions. She obviously wasn't there for the colon. "Hey, buddy," I said, "the, uh . . . exhibit doesn't open until 10:00. You want to get a donut?"

"Do they have a *Dunking Donuts*?" he asked, taking the bait.

"Right up ahead," I said as I steered the stroller into line and ordered us each a colon-clogging, fat-filled donut. I needed to kill some time. Plus I didn't really want to be milling around like groupies or pie-eyed tourists waiting for the *Colossal Colon* to open. It's weird enough that we're here in the first place. We don't need to look like rabid fans of the *Colossal Colon*, camping out to be the first one through every morning, and collecting the "I Crawled at the Mall" stickers they hand out, keeping them in a photo-album next to repeated snapshots of us emerging from the colon, smiling and happy.

Shortly after 10:00 we waddled down the hall to the commons area. As it turns out, the *Colossal Colon* has a name—"Coco"—and a fan club. You can purchase a t-shirt that reads, "I © Coco." A theme-design company called Adirondack Scenic that specializes in crafting sets for Hollywood movie studios and other entertainment venues built Coco to exacting specifications. The website, www.colonclub.com, says that, "Actual colonoscopy footage was used to ensure that the features inside the Colossal Colon® are as realistic as possible." Coco can be rented and, at the time of this writing, had appeared in 74 cities in 34 countries.

My son and I waited patiently at the mouth of Coco the *Colossal Colon* for our turn as if it was an amusement park ride. A few other older fathers lingered around with their kids, chatting it up with the nurses. My first indication that this might not be quite what I expected came when I heard one man proudly announce, "That's what I had," to his older daughter.

"I always wondered what it looked like," he said and his daughter gave him a hug.

He seemed so happy and proud. He had the self-conscious glow of a survivor; and I realized how this thing, bizarre as it might have seemed, served other purposes beyond awareness. It allowed people to confront their cancer, their mortality, and to grieve, perhaps even gloat over their efforts to fight off the attack. It was like seeing your nemesis on display, captured and contained for public viewing.

When our time came, my son and I donned the blue paper booties and entered into the reddish-pink tube. It was about 4 feet in diameter and cramped enough that I had to crawl, while my son could walk upright most of the way. The walls were made of some kind of polymer or plastic compound—the kind of thing they use in museums to make fake rocks or in zoos to create natural-looking artificial habitat, and in mall playgrounds to make slides and climbing walls. The floor was padded with foam, which protected my knees from the hard ridges and bumps of the lower intestine.

Our first stop was Crohn's Disease. "See how it eats away the lining of your intestine," I said, pointing to the recessed scars and pockmarks that looked like they'd been carved with a blowtorch.

"Ooo, Daddy, look at this," he said excitedly, already moving ahead of me, down the intestinal tunnel. "What is it?" he asked, pointing at a bulbous growth.

"Oh, boy! That's a pre-cancerous polyp," I said. "Feel it."

My son rubbed his hand over the protruding, reddish lump and smiled.

A little further down the tunnel, the light faded and we reached the early stages of colon cancer. A thick red bloom of tissue sprouted into the tunnel and oozed out a hole in the roof.

"Doesn't it look like a volcano, Daddy?" he said as he stood straight up and poked his head out of the hole.

"Yeah, it does actually. Sort of like lava, huh?"

"Yeah, like lava," he said and moved on.

I sat there, rubbing my hands over the lumpy lava landscape, trying not to think that this is what my colon might look like some day, what it might look like today. According to the American Cancer Society, colorectal cancer has a mortality rate of close to 50% with approximately 130,000 new cases diagnosed every year. The Colon Cancer Foundation estimates that roughly 10% of these cases, or 13,000 men and women under the age of 50 will be diagnosed with colon cancer.

I exited the *Colossal Colon* tunnel, stumbling into the bright lights of the mall, and circled around the outside of the tunnel, admiring the realistic replicas of all the stages of cancer. As I waited for my son to go through the tunnel again, I casually rubbed my hands over Coco's external hemorrhoids and wondered if I'd made a mistake bringing him here. If I did, I hoped it was the kind of mistake that makes me a good, if not imperfect father. There is a fine line, I realized, between scarring your children for life and sculpting their identities in odd and interesting ways.

I had no way of knowing that his pre-school teacher would later approach me with concern and inform me that my son, "keeps talking about his colossal colon," or that he would soon be able to list all the parts of the digestive system and draw them on his magnetic doodle-pad for family, friends, and total strangers.

I wasn't ashamed. I was proud of my boy and his odd obsessions. They just might save me some day. Who knows? I thought perhaps he might grow up to become a gastroenterologist or an oncologist and trace his career path back to the day his father took him to the mall so he could crawl through a 40-foot disease-ridden colon named Coco.

Bear Fetish

"I lay down every night with my 5yr old and 2yr old boys and watch Man vs Wild we recorded. The oldest pretends to be Bear and my 2 yr old says 'Bear eat spider.' Just would like to let Bear know all the hard work he does means lots to his youngest fans."

— posted by "ndngrl" to a
Man vs. Wild public message forum

In Siberia, the cold is so brutal that Bear Gryll's survival knife freezes instantly to his flesh. It can happen, just like the mythical tongue-to-the-flagpole story. My kids and I watched, mesmerized, silent, wondering how Bear would get out of this predicament. This may seem like a strange drama to watch with your children. But it's OK because *Man vs. Wild* is "educational" reality TV. It's good for you and your family.

As a former member of the British Special Forces, Bear boasts an impressive physique, speaks with a charming accent, and oozes puckish charm. More importantly, he makes an effective narrator, a compelling guide through the snowy wilderness. You trust Bear and you want to follow him.

In the midst of a hike through subzero Siberian temperatures, he takes time to stop, look into the camera, and tell you a story about an ice climber in the same area last year who put an ice-screw into his mouth, just to hold it for a second, and it froze instantly to his lips.

"By the time he was done pulling it out, his lips, his tongue, everything was just gushing blood."

It's a graphic and memorable image, one that lingers in your head. *The screw, the mouth, the blood.*

Next Bear shows you his knife frozen fast to his hand. You don't actually see him stick it to his hand. It's just there. And then Bear explains that if he peels it off, it will peel off layers of skin.

Ouch, you think.

Bear has a pretty serious dilemma. And you're still thinking about *the screw, the lips, the tongue, and the gushing blood.* You still have that image in your mind of the ice-climber's wounded mouth.

The only answer to Bear's dilemma is obvious— especially if you've watched Bear in action before.

Bear will have to pee on his hand.

There is clearly no other option, no other way to warm his hand and release the knife from its skin-peeling grip. He can't survive in Siberia with a knife stuck to his hand. As a viewer you understand this. You realize subconsciously that it would be pretty rare for someone to get a survival knife stuck to his hand like that and, because he's given you a different scenario already, you naturally substitute. You resort to what you know.

You know about that ice-climber and that metal screw stuck to his lips. Bear told you about this, gave you this image. And as a fuzzy circle blots out Bear's penis and the urine stream arcs thick and strong, soaking his hand, freeing the knife, you can't help it. Your brain does it. You think of *the screw, the mouth, and the tongue.*

The wet knife slips quietly to the snow below. Bear wipes his hand somewhere, off camera, possibly on his pants; and you are left to wonder what exactly it is that Bear is trying to teach you and your kids.

In the Sahara Desert, water is scarce. That's the point. And if Bear is going to survive jumping out of a helicopter into the Sahara he needs to get all the water he can get. He also needs to keep cool. Bear, of course, is always cool as a cucumber; but we're talking here about temperature, thermometer markings. We're talking heat. A few degrees can make the difference between "life and death."

Again, he is presented with a dilemma.

This time it's not the loss of flesh he's risking, but his life. Stay cool or die. It's amazing to consider what sorts of industrious behavior such a dilemma will inspire or condone. Bear Grylls, for example, removes his shirt and soaks it in urine. Then he carefully wraps the sodden shirt around his head—ostensibly to keep his head a few degrees cooler. He hikes for hours through the sun with the shirt on his head. And he doesn't complain about pee dripping down into his eyes, trickling behind his ears, or running down his back. He doesn't complain about the smell either. Later he will probably drink some of this pee. He will probably squeeze it out of the shirt, directly into his mouth.

In next week's episode, Bear will try to survive in the Scottish Highlands or the Amazon or Alaska or Africa. There is a good chance he will drink pee there too. In just about every single episode of *Man vs. Wild* on the Discovery Channel, Bear Grylls finds some reason to pee on himself, drink his own urine, or at the very least, get naked. It is, I think, pretty clear that in addition to being a hardcore survivalist, he is also a pretty hardcore exhibitionist; and the show is an elaborate staging for what amounts to fulfillment of Bear's sexual fetish fantasies.

Much has been made recently about Bear's propensity for exaggeration and outright fabrication of "life threatening" situations. A YouTube search will provide numerous video clips to illustrate the fiction in Bear's brand of reality TV. But to me, this is not only a boring discussion but it misses the point.

Let's assume the show is all fiction. That doesn't change the fact that the main character in the show spends an inordinate amount of time drinking pee. Or at least pretending to drink pee. This is the truth of what we witness.

I'm not sure which is worse: To drink your own pee or to go to elaborate lengths to make it appear to others as if you are drinking your own pee? The point is that we watch. Millions of us. Parents and their children. We watch because it is a "nature show," a grand adventure, and it seems fun and harmless—like Mutual of Omaha for a new generation.

I know what you're thinking: *Marlon Perkins never peed on himself or Jim. He never drank pee.*

This is true. But we're talking about a new brand of nature television. It's not enough to simply be curious about wild places and fly over them in a helicopter. It was curiosity, after all, that fueled Marlon's efforts to risk Jim's life. No, these days, your experience of wild places on TV is an on-the-ground, in-the-moment dramatic push to survive against the antagonism of nature—an environment so harsh and unforgiving that it would force you to drink pee. It makes for great television, you have to admit. But Bear is driven by much more than curiosity. He is driven to conquer, to summit, to survive; and most of all, to show off his wanker on national television.

Here's the thing, though. For a show mainly about Bear's

wanker, it does have some surprising educational value in places. My kids love it. Not only because we find it hilarious when Bear drinks his pee; but also because Bear does other things that kids love to talk about. In fact, he acts a lot like an undisciplined toddler in the woods—running around naked, putting disgusting things in his mouth, touching his wanker, and getting dirty and wet.

When I watched Bear's show with my kids, I often had to explain that, in fact, you wouldn't want to spend 3 hours carving a bow and arrow to fish for teeny-tiny piranha—despite what Bear tells you about the "Natives" and how they used to do the same—because you would be better off fishing for them with a bit of string and a bug. Or I'd tell them that, despite how fun Bear makes it look, it may not be the best use of energy and survival resources to build a toboggan out of a deer-carcass and scavenged wood for a downhill snow-ride in Siberia.

I might've reminded the kids that, for your average hiker or backpacker lost in the wilderness, there are not too many random and well-placed deer carcasses for you to harvest anyway and you're probably better off just trying to hike down quickly, focus on shelter and water, and leave the handi-crafts for people who have time for sledding and bow-hunting.

The point, though, was that I was teaching them something and so was Bear; which I guess means that in addition to being bizarre fetish porn, *Man vs. Wild* was also truly educational television. I found that, as we watched the show together (and I don't let them watch it alone for obvious reasons), I was able to tell the kids things I learned either in Boy Scouts or from camping with my dad or with their mom, those important lessons about surviving in the wilderness.

Very few of them involved drinking pee.

One day we were visiting my folks after we'd watched Bear's show, and my son decided to tell his grandmother about what he'd seen.

"I watched Bear Grylls," he said, "and I thought, *Oh crap, here it comes*. And you know what?"

"No, what?" my mom asked patiently, having no idea who Bear Grylls is or how much urine he consumes on air.

She would be mortified.

"You can use the sap from a blood sap tree to heal cuts," he said.

"Really? Wow! That's amazing."

She was right. It *was* amazing. My son knew this cool new fact. And it was the image of Bear cutting into that tree, wiping the blood red sap from the wound and smearing into a white paste on his hands, pressing it into tiny cuts and scrapes, that imprinted that lesson into my son's imagination. Trees can heal. Medicine comes from the earth. Sap will save you. And pee is warm enough to free a knife frozen to your flesh. God help any child who sticks his tongue to a flagpole around my kids; because this is the sort of dilemma for which they already know the only reasonable solution.

Five Early Lessons in Parenting

1. HOW TO BE A SUPERHERO

My son came home one day from his progressive and politically correct Providence, Rhode Island, pre-school and informed me that he was not allowed to talk about superheroes.

"Why not?" I asked, flabbergasted. This couldn't be true, I thought. There must be some kind of mistake.

"Because, Daddy," he said patiently, "Superheroes solve their problems by fighting and not with their words."

"Yeah, but . . . ," I tried to respond but couldn't. I was stumped, struck dumb and silent.

He was right. But for Chrissakes, they're superheroes. They're the fabric of childhood. I could barely imagine my own without superheroes. Their stories helped me believe I might actually survive the nuclear 80's. A superhero's problems were not the kind you could just talk about, like parking tickets, traffic jams, or sub-prime mortgages. A superhero had to deal with evil super-villains, rogue mutants, and extra-terrestrial war-mongerers. A superhero had the kind of problems that you might *only* be able to solve by fighting.

One of my favorites, The Incredible Hulk, couldn't even use words. He just grunted, bellowed like an animal, and smashed things. But his anger, his insecurity and pain, *was* his superpower. His existential angst made him special and allowed him to help others with his unique physical gifts.

What better role model for a child of the 80's?

Still I had to admit that my son (or his teachers) had a point. It was just difficult for me to deal with the idea that he could have a superhero-free childhood or, worse yet, that he would think the model of a superhero was this guy on TV named Sportacus.

If you haven't seen an episode of "LazyTown," you're missing one of the most bizarre television experiences. A lot of children's shows are strange, but this one is a truly odd mixture of public service and entertainment. Sportacus, the star of the show, teams up with a spunky little pink-haired girl named Stephanie and a gang of children wearing rubber puppet suits. An adult male outfitted in a tight blue spandex flight-suit and aviator goggles, Sportacus speaks with a faux-French accent and wears a handlebar mustache waxed to sharp points. He champions lifestyle choices like physical activity and eating fruit. Pretty much any problem in LazyTown can be solved with exercise and an apple.

But what good would Sportacus be in the face of real danger? How would he handle a supervillain like Magneto or Lex Luthor or Doctor Octopus? What dreams of survival would he inspire? His beloved fruit would be poisoned with radiation. Exercise is difficult when you have a second head growing out of your shoulder and sort of pointless if you've mutated into a Ninja reptile. LazyTown is yet another reminder that my son lives in a world that is both eerily familiar to and strikingly different from my own childhood reality.

Some days I feel terribly ill-equipped to teach him anything.

After watching the animated film *The Incredibles*, we

had another superhero discussion, about Mr. Incredible's reasons for lifting train cars like dumbbells.

"Why did he do that, Daddy?"

I told him that Mr. Incredible was working out, getting stronger to fight evil, sort of like when Daddy lifts the dumbbells at home.

Then I asked, "Do you think Daddy could lift a train car?"

"Yeah," he said, and with no prompting at all from me, "'Cause you're a superhero."

I just let that one settle in for a while. I let it linger in the rarified air of our minivan.

Then I repeated the story over and over again, telling friends and even strangers. But the more I told it, the more self-conscious I became, the more aware of my own shortcomings as a potential superhero. I have bad knees and bad ankles. My shoulder is wrecked. I'm lactose intolerant. I'm generally afraid of confrontation, and I trust strangers and freaks way too easily. I have more curiosity than common sense. And I look terrible in tights.

I'm glad I didn't ruin the moment, but part of me thinks I should have politely informed him that I am no caped crusader. I'm a regular guy who makes bad choices sometimes, and he probably shouldn't depend on my superpowers to protect him from harm. But then again I figured he'd have the rest of his life to learn this lesson. So I decided to let him believe for a while that I could lift some trains or maybe even—following his example—use my words instead of my fists to save the world and protect my family; because perhaps all children need these sorts of fictions to feel safe.

2. HOW TO PLAY DEAD

When I was five or six a huge scar creased my face, and I towered over many of the other kids. Not only had I pulled a pocketknife on my best friend and booted a kickball through a school window, but I regularly led a gaggle of boys around the playground in a militaristic march, while chanting, "Crush. Kill. Destroy."

I had some issues. But I overcame them. Mostly.

So I wasn't really worried when my son's preschool teacher pulled me aside one day to tell me that he'd been playing a game with the other kids where they put a baby in the oven.

When she said this she said the last part almost in a whisper, *a baby in the oven*. She folded her hands in front of her as if in prayer and stretched her lips out thin like a knife. This was the same teacher I had to talk with about my son's repeated reference to his colon and his drawings of the digestive system. She was one of those preschool teachers who just seemed completely incapable of understanding little boys; but she did get me thinking a bit about where he might have learned such things.

Then I remembered that I'd recently read Hansel and Gretel to him, and let me tell you, that is a seriously dark and twisted story. But I thought about it more and realized there are actually quite a few children's stories about children being shoved into ovens or cooked in pots or cakes. One of our favorites, Sendak's *In the Night Kitchen*, features a naked boy baked in a cake by portly bakers with Hitler moustaches. And then I thought about a game my son liked to play with his mother. It was called "The Baby Bagoo" game, and it was a regular part of our everyday life in Rhode Island. I figured it was the kind of imagination play that good parents are supposed to do with their precocious children.

This is how it went: My son would climb up on the bed and curl into a fetal position. He'd coo and babble like a baby.

Then my wife would walk into the room and say, "Yes, I've come to the orphanage today because I would like to adopt a baby," and then, "Oh, look at all these babies. I want a little girl baby. Where are the little girl babies?"

My son would cry and babble urgently.

"Oh, look at this cute baby!" my wife would say. "Oh, but he's a boy baby."

"Ga. Ga. Ga. Goo. Goo," my son would say.

"What's your name, baby?"

"Baaagoooo."

"Bagoo?"

My son nodded his head.

"Oh, you're such a sweet baby Bagoo. I want to take you home," she said as she wrapped him up and carried him to another part of the room or the bed.

"Now, I'm going to leave you here by the river/ ocean/lake/bathtub, OK, Baby Bagoo? Don't go anywhere."

She'd turn around and Baby Bagoo would promptly roll into the water and go under.

"Oh my god!" she'd yell, "My baby! My baby!" as she pulled him out of the water, limp, eyes closed. "Bagoo? Bagoo? Speak to me. Oh no, my sweet Baby Bagoo is dead."

On cue my son's eyes would flutter and open wide. His arms would begin to flail and he'd rise up, cooing and babbling and saying "Bagoo" over and over again. He would be born again, newly risen, and then we'd go about our normal routines.

Of course I recognized that my son was working

through a lot of fears—layers of fear—with this game. It somehow touched on fear of abandonment, death and water, issues of gender, and the promise of reincarnation. But it was an admittedly strange game, one that other people might not understand. It even freaked me out sometimes.

I never told my son's teachers about Baby Bagoo. I thought they might worry about us. But what they didn't know wouldn't hurt them—unless of course they were hurt by the un-tethered imaginations of children. Our cultural avoidance of death and our ignorance of its meaning begins at an early age. One of the things that makes little kids so morbid, so creative, and so fun to be around is that they are not afraid of death. Or rather they have not yet been taught to face death through fear rather than through curiosity. For my son, curiosity generates questions—and it is these that I'm constantly encouraging him to pursue. "Never stop asking questions," I say in my more parental moments. Fear only leads us into the darkness of easy answers, to avoidance and ignorance . . . and this is usually about the time he stops listening to me.

"Daddy?" my son asked me once at a restaurant.

"Yes?"

"Why do we not like George Bush?"

Silence. The sound of guilty pride. Or the sound of me trying to come up with a reason that would make sense to a four year old, or trying to just pare down the list I keep in my head.

"Is it because he doesn't share his toys?"

For my son, this was the ultimate knock against one's character.

"Kind of," I said.

I was trying to speak his language.

"And because he's fighting a war in the desert and

161

killing people for oil?'

"Uh huh," I said.

I swear I didn't prompt him to say this.

"Daddy?" he said, pausing to blow bubbles in his soda. "Why is he doing that?"

"Good question," I said.

I didn't have an answer either. I also didn't have an answer for why people want to bomb trains or planes or malls or sporting events, or why so many stories are about the loss of innocence. I just knew that we had to keep telling them. And I worried sometimes that fear would rise up and fill the void of answers, that he would stop saving babies from ovens and rivers because someone told him he'd got the story wrong.

3. HOW TO GET RICH

In 2006, shortly after we moved to Fresno, California, I bought my son a frog-shaped sandbox and two hundred pounds of sand from Home Depot. As we were driving home with it in the back, he asked me if I thought a robber would come and steal his sandbox.

I laughed. "I don't think a robber would be interested your sandbox."

"Why not?" he asked.

This made me stop and think. I didn't want to admit that his sandbox wasn't valuable because you couldn't sell it for crack, crank, meth, or a bottle; that it wasn't valuable because you couldn't hock a sandbox or recycle it for cash. Lately, the robbers in Fresno had been targeting street-lights in the nice neighborhoods, pilfering yards and yards of copper wire and selling them to recycling plants. More recently there had been a rash of thefts of catalytic converters from cars parked in driveways and public parking lots. Something about the stuff inside that could be sold on the black market.

My son's sandbox really only had sentimental value. It was not worth money on the black market. It couldn't be resold or recycled easily. But what if there was a black market that trafficked in sentimental value, an underworld where my grandfather's typewriter is worth more than my laptop, or where a child's sandbox is worth more to a meth-head than the copper wiring in the street-lights?

If there were such a market for sentimental value, we'd be rich.

With a few exceptions, most of what we owned was valuable purely for sentimental reasons. We liked our neighborhood, but it was not affluent. There were five vacant, essentially abandoned houses on our block, four of them at our end of the street. Though just one house away from an elementary school, we were also in some gang's territory. I didn't know which one. The only real evidence I could see were graffiti tags on our trash cans. Our neighborhood was not high-crime—mainly because there wasn't much to steal. My son asked us once if we were ever going to be rich, and we gave him our standard line about being teachers and writers and how we were rich in "the things that matter."

I didn't want to say his sandbox wasn't valuable; but I also didn't want him to be afraid of robbers or bogeymen or the people who picked through our recycling bin, looking for bottles and cans. We'd had a few scares recently.

Once when my son and my wife were out walking the dog, they spotted the black-and-white police helicopter—a ubiquitous presence in our neighborhood at night—hovering just a block away. A voice boomed over the chop, ordering someone to "come out now with your hands up"; they hightailed it home.

Another morning, during our regular walk down to the bakery, my son and I passed a corner roped off with police tape. We found out later that a man had fired shots at a police officer, led the police on a high speed chase into someone's yard, crashed his car, and was shot more than 80 times by pursuing officers. I wanted to alleviate my son's fears about a robber stealing his sandbox, but I couldn't pretend that crime wasn't real and I didn't want to tell him his new toy was worthless.

Instead I told him this: "You know what? Your sandbox would probably just be too heavy for robbers to lift. There's two hundred pounds of sand in there," I said. "That weighs almost as much as Daddy."

This was mostly true. I weigh quite a bit more than his sandbox. But it seemed to help. He sat there for a while, perhaps imagining the robbers trying to lift his frog full of sand or his Dad. I often tried to deflect and distract with humor; and I hoped he was imagining me curled up in the frog.

Then he said, "Daddy, I think robbers are golden."

"Golden?" I asked.

"Yeah, I think robbers are golden and have three golden horns."

"Golden horns, huh?"

"And they're made of metal," he said finally.

I imagined tri-tipped monsters of golden metal clanking and clunking through the side gate—a team of them, four or more with shovels, emptying his frog-shaped sandbox into five-gallon buckets they would trade for cash at the asphalt plant; one of them hefting the plastic frog onto his shoulder and dragging the lid across the concrete. I rose from slumber to the sounds of scraping metal and labored breathing. I dialed the police and watched the golden robbers squeeze into a blue van, ducking so their three horns didn't hit the door frame. If I wanted to, I could see them circling the neighborhood, pilfering tricycles, soccer balls, and boxes of sidewalk chalk for their weekly haul to the other black market, the warehouse full of battered toys, worn-out t-shirts, and sagging recliners; shelves piled high with emotional attachments, a warehouse full of the most obscurely valuable things you could imagine. I hoped that if I tried hard enough, I could pretend that all robbers were golden sentimentalists, burdened by their metal skin and their guilt over stealing a child's sandbox; but I knew that if they were, we'd be the target.

4. HOW TO BE A HUMMINGBIRD

Providence, Rhode Island, 2005. The rain had been coming down in sheets for nine days straight, seeping through the walls in our basement, leaving puddles beneath the oil tank. We needed to get out of the house, and we drove fast, just barely tethered to the asphalt, headed for a movie in Massachusetts, a movie about a giant Were-Rabbit ravaging the village gardens. The red and green and yellow lights flowered in the moist fog. They twinkled and blinked intermittently with green. It was too much sometimes, too heavy. This place. This moment in time. The white noise of water-spray competed with the radio voices. My son blithely chattered away in his car-seat, conversing with his invisible friend, Tum-Tum the elephant.

Meanwhile my wife and I talked openly about recent bomb threats to subways in New York City. We said whatever we wanted—things like, "bound to happen," and "nothing we can do," or "just gets worse and worse." We admitted that this was our reality now. But a claymation movie about a giant Were-Rabbit awaited us, and we were happy about this. We were out of the house and not thinking, just driving and living. We were good Americans. It was early October, 2005, and we'd already decided not to go to New York before the bomb threats were issued—mainly because we couldn't afford the trip. But when we'd heard the reports of threats to subways and public transit, we were both honestly relieved to be anywhere but the city.

"Can you imagine that?" my wife asked, responding to another NPR update on the car radio.

"Getting bombed?" I asked.

"Yeah," she said. "Or living with that threat every day like they do in so many other places."

"No, no I can't imagine."

I suddenly realized that our son had gone silent; and the moment began to stretch and expand, distended with silence. He was listening to everything we'd said. He was paying attention to all the words and possibilities, looking for the suggestion of violence or fear or conflict because he had Doppler radar for such drama.

"Who's getting bombed, Daddy?" he asked.

"Nobody, honey," my wife said, "Daddy and Mommy were just talking . . ."

"It's a figure of speech," I chimed in, but I was kidding myself.

He understood. He listened to NPR every morning and heard me ranting at the voices. I didn't want him to be afraid of war and bombs. I didn't want him to feel targeted. I wanted him to stay young and innocent and fearless as long as possible. But I also didn't want to shelter him from the truth or from real danger. I had to prepare him to live in a world where people bombed trains or sporting events or buildings. But how was I supposed to do this? I was in the midst of a full-on parental pause, a seizure of language, and I didn't know what to say.

Then my wife swooped in with this diversion: "What do you want to be when you grow up?"

He paused for a moment, letting the possibilities balloon.

"Hmmmm, " he said, "Maybe a hummingbird."

April 15, 2013, Fresno, California: My son the hummingbird, born almost nine months after 9/11, will soon turn eleven. He's just a few years older than Martin Richard, the youngest victim of the Boston Marathon bombing. My son is a bright boy who takes painting lessons, plays the trombone, and dreams of being a filmmaker. He still likes birds but he doesn't want to be one when he grows up. His mother now has a house a few blocks away from me. My son and his sister live with me half-time, splitting the weeks. Things have changed a lot in eight years. But my son tells me that he still likes listening to NPR in the car because he learns cool things. These days he's been listening to the news of the Boston Marathon bombing and the subsequent manhunt with what appears to be a kind of careful detachment, a calculated pre-adolescent disinterest. But he knows all the details, knows the bombs were packed in pressure cookers, knows they blew apart peoples' legs, and he knows the bombs killed a young boy.

My five-year-old daughter seems mostly oblivious to the news; she makes up songs in the back seat as we drive from school to home and listen to the radio reports. She doesn't ask the same questions that my son asked years before, but I know from experience that she's listening. I know she's absorbing it all. And I suppose that's what I'm reminded of every time something like this happens. Such things—these bombings, this terror—have the capacity to shrink your reality down to what really matters, making the world seem tiny and impenetrable, while simultaneously expanding things exponentially until your world seems immense and fragile and impossible to maintain.

I was still a new parent when my son first became aware of bombs, when he first started to ask "why" questions about war and violence. I can't say that I know a lot more now than I did then. But perhaps *he* knew something then that we can all try to remember.

He may have been small, but he thought big and wild and in ways I aspired to match, ways that I still hope to preserve in my daughter and myself. If I could, I'd take them both out in the yard the next time a bomb or some other violence tears through the fabric of our days. Just the three of us, our faces pressed up close to the flowers, and I'd tell them to remember the nectar, remember their wings, their imaginations, and the way they can beat against the pull of violence. It's a simple matter of defying gravity. I want to free them and protect them with this one fact: a hummingbird can beat its wings seventy times in one second. A simple blur of breath and flesh, and they could be gone.

5. AFTER SCHOOL LESSONS

The other father schooled me during first-grade pick-up time.

"Saw some local fauna in the backyard," he said and kind of rolled up on the balls of his feet. He had the tanned muscled calves of a postal worker or a soldier, someone who'd walked a lot of ground.

"An opossum," he said, nodding his head. "The wife wanted me to kill it, but I said, 'No, let it be.'"

I told him and another mom about the raccoon I'd seen crossing busy VanNess Avenue and the Coopers hawk that took down a grackle on our street corner.

I'd called my kids to the window. "Hurry," I said, "check this out," and we watched the hawk stomp on the smaller bird, plunging its talons into the heart, puncturing the tiny chambers until the grackle bled out and stopped shuddering and flapping. It took a long time for that little bird to die. And then we watched the hawk carry it away.

When I finished my story, the mom gasped, "Oh, dear. I don't know . . . ," She put her hand up to her throat, covering the scar where she'd had her thyroid removed. "I can't even . . ."

"It's not violent," I said. "It's natural. The order of things."

In one hand, the other father clutched a snack baggie stuffed with fruit. Strawberries and grapes, maybe a raspberry or two. A gift for his daughter. A treat for the walk home. He brought her something special every day.

"I freaked my sister out," he said, gesturing toward me with the fruit baggie.

The children had already begun streaming out the doors, single-file, gravitating toward parents or guardians, gathering on the grass to wait.

"I poured salt on a block of dry ice," he said over the chaotic noise of children.

"Watch," he'd said to his sister. "Wait for it."

And the deer did come. Two of them. Put their tongues to the salt. Stuck there, they pulled against the dry ice. Anchored to the lick, they strained to break free. And I wanted to tell him to stop.

"And my sister was like, 'What are you going to do

to them?"

I could see the deer pulling on their tongues, practically yanking them from their skulls. Panicked, they must have strained against their own anchor.

The other father handed his daughter the fruit baggie, "Here you go, honey," he said and then he finished his lesson:

"And I was like, 'Oh, I'm not doing nothing,' and that's when I slit their throats."

He smiled, nodding his head again. There was a breeze that day. Unusual for Fresno. But it could not carry his words away. They dropped into the space between us.

The children flocked to their parents, gathering around us like metal fragments to a magnet. Drawn to our shelter. And I wanted to hold them all, to drag them all away from the image of the deer pulling against their tongues, their throats spilling blood.

The other father's daughter looked up at him, his words hanging there, waiting to attach and take root. My own daughter, oblivious to the gore, grabbed my hand and begged, "Can I?" pointing at the playground; so I let her go, watching her legs kick up, bouncing toward the cedar chips.

His daughter watched, too, staring at the other girls at play. She wrapped her arms tight around the baggie and squeezed until it burst. *Pop!* Like a shot. And the fruit spilled down around her feet. Grapes rolled like they were trying to escape. The strawberries just sat there, wet and seedy on their flat-cut sides. And the girl looked up at him.

"Why did you squeeze it?" the other father asked, squatting to the concrete, sitting back on the heels of his Army boots.

"I don't know," the girl said, talking into her chest

and twisting her toe on the ground.

"Consequences, baby," he said. "Consequences," as he picked up the fruit, and tossed it into the grass for the squirrels.

Overpass Into Fog

One winter morning after dropping my daughter at daycare, I took the 180 overpass arching into thick fog and, though I knew it well, I couldn't in that moment be sure where the road actually ended. Suspended between past and future, I disappeared into language and place, weather and love, and I wondered how close I'd come to flying totally untethered, released from the bonds of concrete reality. The path behind was already gone, lost in clouds and vast sheets of gray wool weather; and the freeway ahead only unveiled itself one moment at a time, a swiftly passing window that, if you flew too fast, you'd outrun, maybe miss a car next to you, a chance at clarity, or run the risk of slipping off the edge into air and the hard reality of landing. My own car—thumping with metal at high volume, coffee mug rattling in the cup holder—seemed suspended then in an eternal present on the 180, between the lines, where already I'd forgotten how my daughter, only three-years-old, had blurted out, "Goddamnit," from the backseat, and how, as we pulled into the school parking lot, I told her she shouldn't say things like that, Daddy shouldn't say things like that, and then from nowhere it seemed, she also recalled a time when, weeks or months before, I'd been angry at someone parked in front of our driveway and I'd cursed and scared her with a quick storm of words, a micro-burst of anger that belonged elsewhere; but on the overpass, with the light outside the car so hazy and diffuse, I wanted to hold tight, to remember what I said next, that sometimes Daddy lets the little things bother him, sometimes feels angry and frustrated at the small stuff because it's easier than trying to change the big stuff, but that he shouldn't do this, should never scare his daughter with words, and that he's sorry for the clouds, sorry for the unpredictability of his moods these days. After an outburst she'll often ask me, "Are you happy again, Daddy?" And that's a hard question to answer given the current weather in my life. At the park a few days later she will make me a birthday cake from sand. I'll blow out the twig candles and eat the whole fragile thing in front of her. And if we continue to jump forward through time, weeks later, and settle beneath a similar sun in a different park, perhaps emerging from this long fog, I can see myself again, walking a narrow path, skirting a ridge like a wall, watching my feet fall behind another's, a smile overtaking my face because above the two of us a red tail hawk whirls in the thermals and I feel something close to peace. It's just two people finding a new path. Walking quietly. Below the hills a white egret will spin across the green marsh flats, bursting in my vision like a firework in the night; and I will be sure that the blue has never been so bright and low, the whole weight of the sky hanging just over our heads as if we are children beneath a parachute. My son tells me, "There is no present, Daddy. Technically, everything is the past and everything is the future." But at least for this moment on the 180 expressway, perhaps I can stay suspended in the present on the overpass into fog, the memory of our conversation on cursing, my daughter's gambol around *goddamnit* lingering in the penumbral past, as I sail off blindly into the deep abyss of being a divorced father of two children, catching mere glimpses of clear thoughts through windows in the haze; and perhaps such suspension will help me remember that it's important not to pass over such moments, to stay in the vehicle of metaphor, moving forward, even if you can't see the edges or the end, even if the concrete seems to disappear into gray ether, into a terrifying and ecstatic final separation.

ACKNOWLEDGMENTS

I'd like to gratefully acknowledge the literary journals that first published the essays in this book:

"Deep Down in the Country Boy Mine," in *The Pinch*
"Next Stop, Meteor Crater," in *Fourth Genre*
"High Maintenance," in *Mt. Hope*
"I'm Just Getting to the Disturbing Part," in *Fourth Genre*
 Section 1 of "Wake Up Calls," in *Phoebe*
"Into the Mild," in *Terrain.org* (published under the title, "Into the Half-Wild")
"Bright Orange Fear," in *The North American Review*
"The Colossal Colon," in *Waccamaw*
"Bear Fetish," in *The Evolutionary Review*
Parts of "Five Early Lessons in Parenting," in *River Teeth* and "Oh, Baby," from InFact Books
"After School Lesson," in *The Southeast Review*
"Overpass into Fog," in *Brevity*

This book has been a long time in the making—nearly twenty years—and it exists largely because of the support of friends, family, writers, and editors. Michael Steinberg, one of the founding editors of the journal, *Fourth Genre*, not only published the title essay but anthologized it and supported me as an emerging writer many years ago. He's been a champion of my work and the work of many essayists and I'm eternally grateful to him. Rob Shufelt shows up in my writing a lot because he's always been there since we met over thirty years ago. Many of these essays were some of my first publications and I'd like to thank all of the editors who took a chance on these pieces. You changed my life. I'd also like to acknowledge my long-time friends and co-editors, Sophie Beck and Matt Roberts; my colleagues in the MFA Program at Fresno State, Connie and John Hales, Randa Jarrar, Tim Skeen, and Jefferson Beavers; my colleagues in the Department of English at Fresno State and in the low-residency MFA Program at Sierra Nevada College; my current and former Deans, Saul Jimenez Sandoval, Jose Diaz, and Vida Samiian; my amazing students in the MFA Program in Creative Writing at Fresno State; and James and Coke Hallowell for supporting my work with the Hallowell Professorship in Creative Writing. Most importantly, I'd like to thank my family for their support and presence in my work, particularly my children, Sophie and Malcolm and my wife, Andrea Mele, my parents, Sally and John Ramage, Ed and Carolyn Church, and Jim and Debbie Mele. Many thanks also to Patrick Madden, Jerald Walker, Brian Turner, Beth Ann Fennelly, David Ulin, and others for their support and encouragement. It has been a real joy working with Jon Roemer and Outpost19 on this and other projects and I'm very happy that this book found a home with them.

Steven Church is the author of *The Guinness Book of Me: a Memoir of Record, Theoretical Killings: Essays and Accidents, The Day After The Day After: My Atomic Angst,* and *Ultrasonic: Essays* and *One with the Tiger: Sublime and Violent Encounters between Humans and Animals.* His essays have been published in *Passages North, DIAGRAM, Brevity, River Teeth, The Rumpus, AGNI, The Pedestrian, Colorado Review, Creative Nonfiction, Terrain.org,* and many others. He is a Founding Editor and Nonfiction Editor for the nationally recognized literary magazine, *The Normal School*; and he coordinates the MFA Program at Fresno State.

CPSIA information can be obtained
at www.ICGtesting.com
Printed in the USA
BVOW11s1316070518
515500BV00003B/475/P

9 781944 853457